# A Parents Resource Guide to COLLEGE

*With a Special Section on*

### Bill Osher, Ph.D.
### Karen Kellogg, Ph.D.

*Georgia Institute of Technology*

**KENDALL/HUNT PUBLISHING COMPANY**

4050 Westmark Drive        Dubuque, Iowa 52002

# CONTENTS

# Georgia Institute of Technology Resource Guide 125

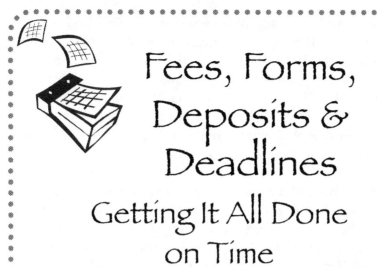

# Fees, Forms, Deposits & Deadlines
## Getting It All Done on Time

College is a milestone for your son or daughter. (S)he is leaving home, making new friends, confronting new ways of thinking, and preparing for a career. (S)he is becoming a new person—an independent, self-sufficient adult. It's easy to forget that college is also a milestone for you. You're losing a member of the household. There will be an empty seat at the dinner table and one less person to help with the dishes. You will have fewer arguments. You will also have fewer conversations. You must learn to love in a new way. You must let go.

Sending a student to college is also a large project to manage. College is expensive. How will you pay for it? There are endless forms to complete and a number of deadlines to meet. There are dozens of decisions: what to buy, what to take, where and with whom to live, and how to get there.

This resource guide will help you with these tasks—letting go psychologically and moving in physically. Both tasks—the psychological and the practical—are important. Your first concerns, however, will be practical ones. Therefore, the first seven chapters of this resource guide tell you how to get your student organized, packed, transported, moved in, and registered. This book will tell you what offices can help, what questions to ask, and what to discuss with your student before (s)he leaves for school. There are important checklists, timelines, and phone numbers.

The next four chapters are about your changing role as a parent. While you must let go, you cannot abandon. How do you walk the fine line between interference and neglect? How do you parent from a distance? While there are no magic rules, there are general guidelines which will help you and your student to negotiate the transition as smoothly as possible. Also included in this guide is a glossary of terms and a bibliography. Most importantly, the last section of this resource guide contains information specific to the college your son or daughter will be attending.

Congratulations! You and your student are about to pass an important milestone.

## Top Ten Things to Do and Deadlines to Meet

Once your student has decided on a college there are many important things to take care of—here are the top ten:

1. Inform the Admissions Office you're coming! The college will require a deposit (usually by May 1) to guarantee a spot in the freshmen class—don't forget to send it in!

2. As a family, complete financial aid papers and mail them into the school as soon as you can. Don't forget to apply for scholarships and grants, as well. The deadline for applying for national financial aid is March 1. See Chapter 2 for more details.
3. Complete a housing contract and pay a deposit. Your student will definitely want to get a space guaranteed, maybe preference a roommate, or preference a residence hall—so send in the housing deposit as soon as you can! This is usually due May 1—the day students should have made a decision on the college they want to attend.
4. Complete a dining contract. Usually, colleges will ask students to sign-up for a meal plan for the dining hall. The meal plans may be based on a specific number of meals (e.g. 10 or 14 meals per week) or on specific dollar amounts per semester/quarter. Have your student think about his/her eating habits carefully before (s)he sends back the contract.
5. All schools require some type of medical form stating that your student has received the proper vaccinations. Many schools won't let students register for classes until this form has been turned in, so make sure to return this form before your student registers for classes. And, although it's not fun, if your student needs additional vaccinations, get them **before** mailing the health forms to the college.
6. Your student should receive information about new student and parent/guardian orientation that will be held in summer or fall. Orientation is critical to student success the first few weeks of school. It's usually first-come, first-serve, so complete the orientation materials ASAP. Also, don't forget these dates when you plan your family vacation. See Chapter 4 for more information.
7. Ask your student's high school to send a copy of your student's final transcript to the Admissions Office. This is required for final acceptance and enrollment, so don't forget!
8. Send all AP credit scores and transcripts that your student earned from another college or through joint enrollment.

This is important for your student's academic adviser. You want your student to get credit for everything (s)he can!

9. If the college requires students to purchase a computer, be on the look-out for great bargains! The college should provide specific hardware or software requirements.
10. The college will notify you when tuition and fees are due. At some schools, classes are dropped if tuition is not paid on time. Do NOT forget to pay tuition and fees by the due date!

---

# We Can Help:
# Campus Resources and Information

Each campus has many offices, each with specific roles. It can be overwhelming trying to keep them all straight. To help you, we have included a list of the most commonly used agencies on campus and a list of their services. Keep in mind that each college may have a different name for these departments or a slightly different function, but these should be close.

**Academic Adviser**—advises students on classes to take

**Academic Departments**—academic advising; faculty offices; changing majors

**Admission's Office**—recruits and admits new students; sends out general information about the college

**Bookstore**—text books; school supplies; computers and computer supplies; paperbacks; stationary; gifts; personal items; college clothing

**Bursar's Office**—tuition and fee payment

**Bus**—many campuses have shuttle vans or buses that can take students around campus and in some cases, around town

**Campus Computing**—activates computer accounts; trouble-shooting; e-mail

**Campus Police/Public Safety**—law enforcement; safety education; escort service; bike registration

**Campus Recreation**—intramurals; weight room; swimming pool; exercise facility

**Career Center**—career counseling; on/off-campus job postings; resume help; job search techniques; interviews with recruiters; placement

**Counseling Center**—counseling for emotional, academic, personal and relational problems

**Dining Services**—meal plans; special dietary needs

**Disabled Student Services**—support services for students with physical or learning disabilities; testing; transportation; ADA coordination

**Financial Aid**—financial planning; scholarships; work study; grants; loans

**Health Center**—medical care; health education; immunizations; women's health care; x-rays; allergy shots; laboratory tests; pharmacy; health insurance; dental (limited to colleges with dental schools)

**Housing Office/Residential Life**—housing contracts; roommate assignments; educational programming; room repairs

**Identification Card (ID)**—checking out library books; campus recreation center; dining hall meal plans; computer labs; athletic events; debit card at the bookstore; heath center; discounts in community business and restaurants

**Learning Resource Center**—study skills; tutoring

**Minority Affairs**—programs to ensure the success of minority students

**Orientation Office**—plans new student and parent orientation programs

**Parking Office**—parking permits; tickets

**Registrar's Office**—academic records; transfer credit; advanced placement credits; registration; grades; residency; graduation

**Student Affairs/Life/Services**—discipline; family emergency support; all activities outside of academics

# Show Me the Money
## Financing College

There are several important issues for parents and students to discuss. Aside from bankruptcy or a life of indentured servitude, how will you cover all the bills? Hopefully, you and your student have decided how to pay for college expenses. If not, there are many options for you to explore. Here is a short summary of your options:

## Ways to Pay for College

### Family Money & Savings

Some people start saving when their children are born, others start later. Determine the family savings. If you have money set aside for college, use it.

### Loans

Loans are borrowed money that students must repay with interest after graduation. Loans can be obtained from college or federal sources. Most loans must begin repayment within six months of college graduation. Loan payments can be deferred for graduate study, loss of job, or other extreme situations. Most banks/federal loan offices will work with students if they are having difficulty paying back a loan after graduation.

## Grants/Scholarships

Grants/scholarships are monies that don't have to be paid back. Individuals, companies, or institutions may offer grants to college students. Grants/Scholarships can be donated by individuals (alumni) or organizations (Elks Lodge). Some scholarships and grants can be for a semester, others could be for several years. Be aggressive and exhaustive in your search for grants and scholarships. You'd be surprised at all the money that is out there—waiting for a student like yours to get!

FOR MORE INFORMATION ON SCHOLARSHIPS, TRY THESE WEB SITES:

www.t3cyber.com/scholarships.html—scholarship and financial aid information

www.novakint.com/SSAC—scholarship and financial aid information

www.fastweb.com—to search for scholarships

www.taj.com/~consltnt/college—scholarship and grant information

www.collegeplan.org—scholarship and grant information

www.scholarshipbook.com/index.html—scholarship information

www.yahoo.com/Education/Financial_Aid/Scholarship_Programs—scholarship information

http://allstar-ent.com/vendor/untitled—scholarship and grants

## Work-Study

The work-study program is an opportunity for students to work on-campus to help pay for school expenses. Work-study jobs are often jobs set aside for students with more severe need. Qualified students are given the opportunity to apply for work-study after their financial need has been assessed by their college or university. The Financial Aid Office can assist you and your student with all your work-study and financial aid questions.

## Other Job

Many college students have a part-time job. With college costs rising, families are asking their college students to help pay for some of their expenses. The most obvious type of job is one at the college or university. The dining services, residence halls, library, and campus recreation departments all depend on student workers. Academic departments and offices all over campus have jobs available for students who can type, file, answer phones or run errands. Many students prefer campus jobs to off-campus jobs because the staff supervisors are aware of the student's needs and are often more flexible when scheduling hours or time off.

If your student wants part-time work, encourage a career-related job if possible. Career-related work in college will be a huge plus for post-graduation career success. It's better for an advertising major to work as a receptionist in an advertising office than to sweep floors at a fast food chain. Refer to Chapter 10 for more information on career planning.

# ✐ Applying for Financial Aid

To apply for financial aid, a student must complete the Free Application for Federal Student Aid (FAFSA) as soon after January 1 as possible, but no later than June 30. Many colleges have an earlier deadline so be sure to check! However, your taxes from the previous year must be completed before the FAFSA can be submitted. The FAFSA asks questions about financial need, ability to pay, and your family situation. The application is free and can be obtained on the internet or from the college or university your student will attend. In addition, students may need to file additional forms to receive a Federal Family Education Loan (FFEL), Stafford Loan or a PLUS Loan. After the FAFSA is mailed and processed, your student will receive a Student Aid Report (SAR) in the mail. You will be asked to check the SAR for accuracy and supply some additional information. Then, mail the SAR back and wait to hear from the college or university as to what aid will be available to your student.

Most likely, the college will require the completion of an additional financial aid form. This can be obtained at the Financial Aid Office of the college or university. These forms must be submitted each year.

FOR MORE INFORMATION ON FINANCIAL AID, TRY THESE WEB SITES OR PHONE NUMBERS:

> www.finaid.org—general financial aid information
>
> www.ed.gov/offices/ope/express.html—to complete a FAFSA on-line
>
> www.fafsa.ed.gov—FAFSA on-line
>
> www.ed.gov/finaid.html—federal aid program information
>
> www.fedaid.com—federal financial aid information
>
> www.collegeboard.org/finaid/fastud/html/intro/html—to figure financial need
>
> 1-800-4-FED-AID (1-800-433-3243)—information on federal student aid

## Spending Money

While tuition, room and board are costly, unfortunately, it doesn't end there. How much does (s)he really need? There are some expenses that occur each semester/quarter: tuition, fees (technology fee, student activities fee), room and board, air fare/bus ticket home, campus parking permit and text books. Here are some additional expenses to plan for: school supplies, laundry, transportation (gas, bus, taxi cab or subway), long-distance telephone calls, stamps, computer disks, clothing, personal care items (soap, toothpaste, etc.), snacks, meals not covered by meal plans, and entertainment.

## Setting a Budget and Sticking to It!

While the amount of discretionary spending for a college student may seem small, creating and maintaining a budget can be an excellent learning experience. Before your student leaves for college, it is wise to sit down and negotiate a budget. By this time, you probably have discussed financing college. Many parents/guardians agree to pay for the big expenses (tuition, room, fees, board, books) and ask their student to pay for entertainment and other incidentals.

Whatever you have worked out with your son/daughter, definitely set a budget. For some students, this is their first time in charge of spending. It can get out of hand if they're not prepared. With your student, make a list of all potential expenses and how much each expense will cost per month. If the total amount is more or less than you had originally anticipated, negotiate a budget that you can both be comfortable with. In your budget, be sure to leave some money for miscellaneous expenses. An easy way for students to keep track of expenses is by using a spreadsheet on a computer. The spreadsheet will allow him/her to permanently categorize and keep track of expenses.

HERE ARE SOME COMMONLY USED FINANCIAL SOFTWARE PROGRAMS:

- Quicken
- Microsoft Money
- Simply Accounting
- QuickBooks Pro

## Checking Accounts

Perhaps the easiest way for college students to maintain their money is with a checking account. Most campuses either have a credit union on campus or a bank nearby. It may be smart to find out the type of ATM machine(s) on campus so your student can set up his/her checking account with that bank. Banks located near college campuses often have special plans for students, such as free checking and a low minimum balance. You can open a checking account when you visit for orientation or when you arrive in the fall.

The location of a checking account (home vs. school) is important for students who live a great distance from campus. If you will be giving your student money on a regular basis, it may be easier for him/her to get a checking account at home so you can make the deposits. The downside of a hometown bank is that an out-of-state or out-of-town check may not be accepted in stores located in campus towns. The other option is mailing checks to your student and having him/her deposit the checks in an account near campus. Many banks also offer check cards that can be used in addition or instead of writing checks. This may be more convenient for college students.

## Credit Cards

Credit cards can be lifesavers in case of an emergency. They are also handy for paying for air fare home, books and other large expenses. The downside of credit cards is that the spending can get out-of-control! Be sure to talk with your student about the dangers of using credit cards. If your student will be using your cards, make sure to set some guidelines. If you are concerned about your son or daughter having too much freedom with your credit card, have them apply for their own. Most credit card companies will give cards to college students and will set a low limit ($300–500). By having a credit card of their own, students can learn the importance of paying off their balances and can build up a credit rating at the same time.

# Where to Live?

## Campus Residence Halls

**M**any college freshmen live in residence halls, and some schools require freshmen to live on campus. There are several advantages to a home on campus. Today, most college residence halls are more than just a place to sleep. They are living-learning communities. Most have a resident or community advisor on each floor and a graduate or professional staff member living in each building. These staff members are responsible for planning social and educational programs for their residents. They also work hard at getting the residents of each floor to know each other. Often times, this is done through block seating at football games, creating floor intramural teams and planning floor social events.

We recommend that freshmen live on campus. It allows new students to adjust to the school without the hassles of maintaining a household. New students have enough to worry about without cooking, cleaning and washing dishes. Laundry facilities are also readily available in each residence hall. By living on campus, students will be surrounded by people their own age and have an easier time making friends. Another advantage of living on campus is that students are more likely to get involved in campus activities and find out about campus opportunities. Refer to Chapter 5 for details on residence hall living.

## Greek Houses

If your son or daughter pledges a fraternity or sorority, there is a possibility that s(he) could move into the fraternity/sorority house the first year. Many colleges will allow students to break their residence hall contracts in order to move into a fraternity or sorority. However, not all institutions have that policy, and, if a contract is broken, you may have to pay a substantial portion anyway.

One advantage to moving into a Greek house the first year is that the cost of room and board may be less expensive. Also, your son or daughter will be living with people who share common interests and may have an easier time adapting to college life. For more information on Greek life, see Chapter 6.

## Off-Campus Apartments

We generally do not recommend traditional age freshmen (17–19 years) live in an off-campus apartment. Approximately 25–30% of all college students live off campus and most are upperclassmen. Students in apartments are isolated from campus and have a more difficult time acclimating themselves to campus. While this may be ideal for upperclassmen, first year students need to make friends, get involved and experience college life. The challenges of an apartment (rent, utilities, cooking, cleaning, driving on campus) are often too much for a first-year student who is going through so many changes already. After all, who wants to cook if someone will do it for you?

## Living at Home

Just under one-half of all college students live at
home with their parents/guardians. The most
obvious advantage for living at home is the money
saved from not paying room and board. Remember that students who commute must pay for
campus parking and quite often, food during the
day. Another advantage for living at home is the
peace and quiet that students have when they need to study or
write a paper.

The biggest disadvantage for students who live at home is their
separation from campus life. They miss out on the impromptu
food runs at midnight, the study groups that form on residence
hall floors, and many other social opportunities that arise. If your
student is going to be living at home, make sure you encourage
him/her to spend as much time on campus as possible to become
acclimated to college life and experience all college has to offer.
A compromise might be to have your student live on campus for
one semester or one year and then move home. This way your
student will have the initial opportunity to make friends and
experience campus life to its fullest. Refer to Chapter 11 for more
information on commuter students.

# disORIENTATION?

## Why Orientation?

Colleges and universities plan orientation programs to familiarize students and parents with the campus, school policies, and all the opportunities available on campus. Generally, there are two types of orientation programs:

1. One, two or three-day sessions during the summer.
2. Three or four days before school starts.

There are advantages and disadvantages to both structures. But, whatever option your student's college offers—plan on attending!

## Students

There are several areas of information that your student will learn about and experience during orientation:

✓ housing
✓ dining
✓ classes
✓ health center

✓ paying fees and tuition
✓ campus policies
✓ campus traditions
✓ social opportunities

- ✓ career planning
- ✓ counseling center
- ✓ student services
- ✓ student organizations
- ✓ Greek life
- ✓ academic departments
- ✓ ID card

## Parents/Guardians

An orientation for parents/guardians is important because college administrators know that your family is in transition, and they want to offer information and support to you. During orientation, many colleges have separate program sessions for students and parents. That's not to say you will never be with your

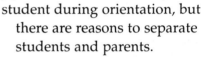

student during orientation, but there are reasons to separate students and parents.

During orientation, students want to see that they can succeed in college. That is why upperclassmen often serve as hosts. Orientation gives incoming students one-on-one time with a current student to find out "what it's really like at college." Your student wants to be seen as independent. Having parents around all the time may make students feel uncomfortable. Be aware of this need, and try to give your student some space at orientation.

Another reason for separating parents and students is that parents will often ask questions on sensitive topics such as campus safety or alcohol which can embarrass students. Conversely, there are some questions that students want to ask but wouldn't ask in front of their parents or guardians. To alleviate parental concerns and avoid student embarrassment, students and parents/guardians are usually separated for some sessions. But relax, you will meet up with your student at least a couple of times before orientation is over.

Finally, there are some parents/guardians who won't let their students make decisions. This is the primary reason that parents are usually not allowed to participate in academic advisement and class registration. Some parents have tried to dominate the advising sessions and tell the student exactly what to major in and what courses to take, regardless of how the student feels. The student would feel pressured to obey Mom and Dad, especially in front of other students or faculty. Before you go to orientation, try to find out your student's preferences for major and the types of courses they want to take. This way, there will be no surprises when your student shows you his/her class schedule.

Most orientation programs will give you time to reconnect with your student during the orientation program. Take advantage of these times to review information, check your list of questions, and set a time and place to meet when the program ends. Be prepared to do a lot of walking during orientation. College campuses can be very spread out, so dress casually and comfortably.

## Other Orientation Options

Some institutions offer additional types of orientation or assimilation programs for students. Many colleges, especially private institutions, offer a type of camp or outdoors experience. These experiences can range from 3 days to 3 weeks in length and usually occur in the summer or immediately preceding the fall semester. They are designed to teach students about campus traditions, get them connected with other students, and to teach them leadership and team building skills.

There may also be orientation sessions for special populations. For instance, if your student has a physical disability, there may be a special orientation to teach him/her about accessibility on campus and where to go for help. Most campuses have some type of orientation for international students and minority students, as well. Non-traditional students and commuter students may also have an orientation session. Check with the institution for information on orientation sessions for special populations.

# There's No Such Thing as a Stupid Question

There will be more information given and presented to you at orientation than is humanly possible to remember. So, to keep the important information organized in your head, make a list of questions before going to orientation. Brainstorm with your student about any and all areas of interest/concern/confusion. Keep a list of questions with you at all times during orientation and cross them off as you get them answered. Here are some important questions to ask:

## Housing/Residential Life

✓ When will we find out about roommates?
✓ What is the size and location of the room?
✓ When is the earliest, latest, and optimal time to move in?
✓ What is the room change policy if there is a room-mate conflict?
✓ What type of accommodations are made for students with disabilities?
✓ Are the rooms wired for computer hook-ups?
✓ Is there voice mail?
✓ Where will they get their mail? How should it be addressed?
✓ Can students stay in their room during spring break, Thanksgiving break or holiday break?
✓ Do students need to insure their belongings?
✓ Can bikes be stored in the winter?

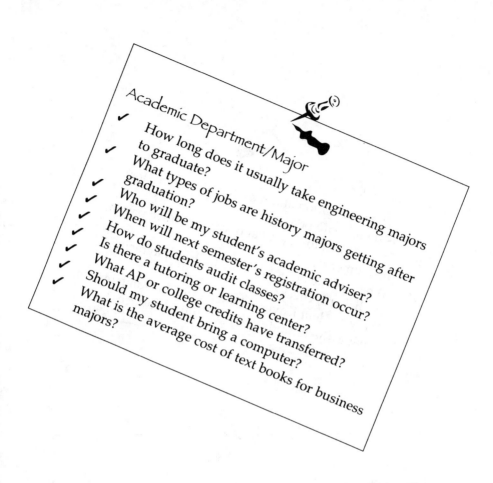

Academic Department/Major

- ✔ How long does it usually take engineering majors to graduate?
- ✔ What types of jobs are history majors getting after graduation?
- ✔ Who will be my student's academic adviser?
- ✔ When will next semester's registration occur?
- ✔ How do students audit classes?
- ✔ Is there a tutoring or learning center?
- ✔ What AP or college credits have transferred?
- ✔ Should my student bring a computer?
- ✔ What is the average cost of text books for business majors?

Health Center

- ✔ Have all the medical forms been received?
- ✔ Can students get allergy shots at the Health Center?
- ✔ Does the school offer student health insurance?
- ✔ Are the campus pharmacy prices cheaper than retail pharmacies?

## Bursar's Office

✓ When are tuition and fees due each semester?
✓ Is there a late penalty?
✓ Do we have to pay all at once, or can we pay in installments?
✓ What are the acceptable methods of payment—credit card, check?
✓ If my student leaves mid-semester for some reason, what is the refund policy on tuition and fees?

## Financial Aid

✓ When is the deadline to apply for scholarships/loans?
✓ What scholarships and grants are available?
✓ When do financial aid checks come in?
✓ What does his/her loan or scholarship cover?
✓ How does loan or scholarship money get applied to his/her account?

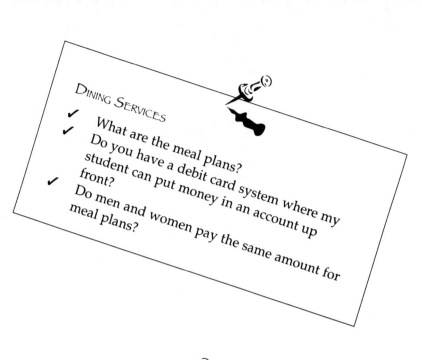

DINING SERVICES

✓ What are the meal plans?
✓ Do you have a debit card system where my student can put money in an account up front?
✓ Do men and women pay the same amount for meal plans?

Career Center

✓ Where can my student go to find a part-time job?
✓ If the part-time job is off-campus, is there any transportation provided?
✓ What kind of placement services are available?
✓ What if my student doesn't have any idea of what he wants to do after graduation?
✓ What is the percent of students that graduate with a job?

Miscellaneous

✓ What help is available for learning or physical disabilities?
✓ Is summer storage available on campus?
✓ Where are some local hotels?

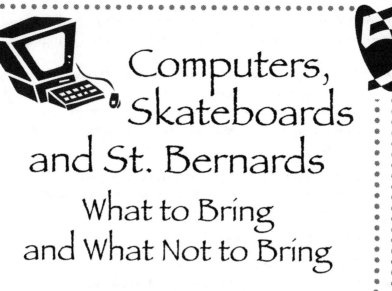

# Computers, Skateboards and St. Bernards

## What to Bring and What Not to Bring

It's hard to know just what to bring to college. Does your student need a car? Will there be a microwave on the residence hall floor? Will (s)he need an answering machine? Whatever your student decides to bring, make sure (s)he contacts the roommate(s) before school starts. The housing office should mail the name and phone number of your student's roommate during the summer. By contacting the roommate(s) ahead of time, they will be able to plan who will bring what (they don't need 2 or 3 refrigerators) and will have a chance to get to know each other before the big day.

## What to Bring

### Clothing

Generally, college students live in jeans, shorts, tennis shoes, t-shirts and sweatshirts. Chances are, they will not be wearing their prom dress or a tuxedo on a weekly basis. However, there are some basic wardrobe essentials every college student should bring:

✓ At least 10 days worth of **socks and underwear**. Doing wash is usually dictated by the number of pairs of underwear left in the drawer. Send enough to allow your student to squeak by a few more days without doing laundry.

✓ Two or three pairs of **jeans**, comfortable pants and/or shorts. Wearing shorts or jeans will vary depending on the climate of the college.

✓ Several **t-shirts**. T-shirts are the staple of a college student's wardrobe.

✓ Two or three **sweatshirts**. Sweatshirts serve multiple purposes for college students: covering up a dirty t-shirt, in place of a jacket at night, easy to throw on after they have overslept and are running late for class.

✓ **Sweatpants**. Sweatpants are great for lounging, studying and exercising. They go well with the sweatshirt when students are running late for class.

✓ Two pairs of running or walking **shoes**. Most students, at any given time, will be wearing tennis or running shoes. In case one pair gets lost or wet, it's handy to have a spare pair.

✓ One or two **nice outfits**. Every so often there is an occasion for college students to dress up: a date, religious service, an event for a student organization or fraternity/sorority. For women, a skirt and dress would be fine. For men, at least one suit or sport coat and tie with nice pants. Don't forget dress shoes to go with the outfits!

✓ A **coat** for every season. Depending on the climate, your student could need a winter coat, rain coat and light jacket. Many students wear light-weight pullovers that they can wear a sweatshirt or t-shirt under as need be.

✓ **Umbrella**. There are many umbrellas that fold up very small and can be tucked into a backpack or book bag. You don't want your student caught in the rain without an umbrella. It's a long walk back to the residence halls.

✓ **Swimsuit**. You never know when your student will be invited to a pool party or take a swimming class!

✓ A set of **old clothing**. There will be at least one activity for which a set of very old clothing will be appropriate, such as: a mud volleyball tournament, intramurals, or a fraternity/sorority philanthropy project.

## Furniture

Don't worry about buying furniture for your student's residence hall room. Generally, the following items are provided in most residence hall rooms.

✓ Bed—per person
✓ Desk—per person
✓ Chair—per person
✓ Drapes/blinds
✓ Waste basket
✓ Closet/drawers
✓ Wall mirror

## Miscellaneous

Besides clothing and personal care items, there are several other items your student will want to bring:

✓ 3–4 sets of towels
✓ Rolls of quarters for washing machines, dryers, soda machines
✓ Shower shoes
✓ Bath bucket for carrying shampoo and soap to the bathroom

- ✓ Iron (optional)
- ✓ 2 sets of sheets, a pillow, a comforter
- ✓ Laundry bag or hamper
- ✓ Drying rack
- ✓ Laundry detergent
- ✓ Pictures from home
- ✓ Drinking cup, bowls, plates, and basic utensils
- ✓ Hangers
- ✓ Camera
- ✓ Radio/CD player/stereo
- ✓ Small refrigerator
- ✓ Small sewing kit
- ✓ Small tool box
- ✓ Adhesive gum for hanging up posters
- ✓ Power strip with surge protector and additional outlets
- ✓ Extension cord
- ✓ Desk supplies
- ✓ Alarm clock!
- ✓ Telephone/answering machine (check with college to see if voice mail is provided)

## Computer

If your student can afford to buy or bring a computer to campus—do it! Increasingly, colleges require their

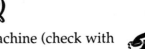

students to bring a computer to campus. If your student does not have a computer, (s)he will have to go to a computer lab. The number of computer labs on campuses varies with the size of the student body. Some campuses have very high computer-to-student ratios (1 computer for every 20 students). Other campuses have low computer-to-student ratios (1 computer for every 100 students). The campus computing department at each school should have that information.

## Advantages for Having Your Own Computer

Some of the best reasons to get a computer are that most professors require work to be done on computers, most people on college campuses use e-mail, and it will save your student a lot of time and energy. With his/her own computer, your student can do the work anytime day or night and they won't have to wait in line at a computer lab for other students to finish.

## Refrigerator

This is a must! Campus dining halls are not generally open 24 hours a day. Having a refrigerator in a room can be a big convenience and, in the long run, a money saver. If your student can stock up on a few essential food items to make him/herself, this will save money on running to fast food restaurants when the dining hall is closed or if your student is sick and cannot get to the dining hall. Most campuses have refrigerator vendors that will sell or rent mini-refrigerators (4.5 cubic feet) on move-in day. They are generally priced from $89 to $119 per year. You can also purchase mini-refrigerators at discount stores. Purchasing your own refrigerator, especially if you have younger children who can use this in the future, can be a better investment.

## Lofts

Many college students prefer sleeping in lofts rather than the standard residence hall beds. Lofts are free standing structures that are placed against a wall and elevate the mattress(es) close to the ceiling. This gives students room underneath the loft for storage or a couch. Again, check with the residence hall staff to see if lofts are allowed and what kind. You can make your own (using dimensions from the housing office) or you may be able to buy one during move-in day from an upper-classman trying to get rid of a loft. Your student should check with his/her roommate on this because they may already have a loft from an older brother or sister!

## Carpet

Check with the housing office to see if the residence hall room is carpeted. If not, your son/daughter will probably want to get a large piece of carpet or some rugs for the room. Cold floors are no fun to step on first thing in the morning! You can get carpet remnants from carpet shops in any town.

## Microwave

Before you purchase a microwave, check with the residence life office to make sure they are allowed. And, check to see if the residence halls have microwaves in lounges or in kitchenettes. A microwave is not as necessary as a refrigerator, but it is definitely a convenience. If your student has special dietary needs or is especially finicky, a microwave can occasionally provide an alternative to cafeteria food. There are also appliances on the market that have a refrigerator on the bottom and a microwave on top. You have two appliances for the space of one.

## Television/VCR

A TV and VCR are not necessities for college students, even though they might think they are. Most residence halls have lounges with TVs/VCRs in them already. So, it really isn't necessary for students to bring them. There is also a danger for the students with TVs in their rooms because they are likely to watch TV instead of studying.

## Answering Machines/Voice Mail

Before your student buys an answering machine, check with the housing office to make sure there is not automated voice mail in the rooms. Many campuses provide this service for students which eliminates the need for answering machines. If voice mail is not available, an answering machine can be a big help when you're trying to reach your student.

# Whether to Bring It

Deciding on what clothes to bring and how many clothes to bring depends on 3 factors:

1. HOW FAR FROM HOME IS COLLEGE? If your student is going to college a short distance from home, (s)he will have easier access to clothing at home. It will be easier to get each season's clothing if it's only a 2–4 hour drive. Bringing one season's worth of clothing at a time will be a good bet for any student living close to home. However, if your student is going a considerable distance, (s)he may need to bring two season's worth of clothing. This really depends on how often you could visit or ship clothing to your student.

2. HOW MUCH CLOSET/DRAWER SPACE WILL THERE BE? This is the million dollar question. But the answer is: not as much space as they'd like! Residence hall rooms are not built for students to bring as much stuff as they can. They are built to hold the basics. Keep in mind that your student will be sharing that minimal drawer/closet space with one, two or even three other roommates. Once your student finds out his/her room assignment, (s)he will need to find out the amount of closet and drawer space. Many schools provide a room layout and dimensions in their housing materials. If this information is not provided, call the housing office or check their web page.

3. HOW IS YOUR STUDENT GETTING TO COLLEGE THE FIRST TIME? If you will be loading up the family truckster or renting a trailer, your student can pack as much as they can fit. However, if your student is flying to college, the number of bags is quickly reduced because of airline regulations. Keep in mind that other bags could be shipped later. It may be cheaper to ship bags via

Greyhound buses or UPS rather than through the mail or over-night mail carriers.

# To Bring a Car or Not?

Deciding whether or not to bring a car will be based primarily on one fact: Will the college allow freshmen to bring cars? Once you find the answer to this question, you can weigh the pros and cons. Many colleges have limited parking spaces, and they are assigned to upperclassmen first. If the college allows first-year students to have cars, most likely they will be parking a great distance from their residence hall room or campus.

If the college prohibits freshmen from bringing cars, they always make exceptions. For instance, if your student has an off-campus job, they may get special permission to bring their car. Also, if your student has a medical condition that interferes with his/her walking, a doctor's note can probably get him/her exempted from the rules.

If your student brings a car, be sure to review the options if there is car trouble. Find out if the campus police will help change a flat tire or give a car a jump start. The safest thing to do may be to join an auto club, such as AAA (1-800-298-5222). This way your student can get help with his/her car 24 hours a day.

## Having a Car on Campus Can Be a Great Advantage

1. Your student will be able to drive home.
2. They will be able to get groceries or run to another store for necessities.
3. They are not dependent on other people for rides home or around town.
4. Your student can drive to work if (s)he has a job off-campus.

## Having a Car on Campus Can Also Be a Disadvantage

1. Other students will ask to borrow the car.
2. Your student can end up paying for gas when several people are riding along.
3. It can be expensive with gas and insurance costs.
4. They will have to pay for a parking permit.

## Paying for Parking

If your son/daughter brings a car to campus, they will have to pay for a parking permit each semester or each year. Colleges vary their costs for parking from $30 per semester to $250 a year. This information should be available at new student orientation, or you could call the college's parking office or look at their web page.

# A Bicycle Built for One

If a car is not an option for your student, a bicycle is an easy and cheaper alternative. Each college will have an area to lock bicycles. These areas will be outside the residence halls and around campus. The price of a bike lock ranges from $15–50, but it's worth the expense. If your student brings a bike to campus, make sure (s)he registers it with campus police in case it is stolen. Bikes can be used to get to class in a hurry and to ride to nearby stores or fast food places. Be sure to check with the college to see how many bikes are stolen each year. If there are hundreds of bikes stolen, you may want to re-evaluate bringing a bike or only bring a bike that is expendable. Top quality, high-priced racing or mountain bikes are prime targets for theft!

# What Not to Bring

There are some definite items that your student should not bring to the residence halls.

## Pets

Most residence halls are not equipped to handle pets. Therefore, most pets are not allowed, including dogs, cats, snakes, lizards, turtles, hamsters and rabbits to name a few. Can you imagine walking a dog down four flights of stairs every time he needs to relieve himself? Also, the smell from pets could be unpleasant to room-mates and others in the building. Some colleges may allow students to have fish in a small fish bowl or aquarium. But, it is often difficult to keep fish because they won't be fed on spring break or holiday break. The best advice is to keep pets at home.

## Firearms/Fireworks/Weapons/Ammunition

At most colleges and universities, firearms or explosives of any kind are not permitted. In addition, ammunition, bows and arrows, hunting knives, sling-shots, num-chucks are usually not allowed in the residence halls.

## Miscellaneous

Quite often, hot plates, space heaters and waterbeds are not allowed in residence halls. In addition, candles, incense burners, halogen lamps or oil lamps are generally prohibited for safety reasons.

# ΔΩΣ To Pledge or Not to Pledge

## Greek Life

D eciding whether or not to join a fraternity or sorority is an individual decision. Being Greek provides students with many unique opportunities and challenges. But before students can join a Greek organization, they must go through a mutual selection process known as Rush. Each college or university conducts rush differently, but, there are similarities that most schools have regarding rush.

## Sorority Rush

The rush process for women consists of a set of daily events. The number of events decreases each day of rush as the sororities and the Rushees (women going through rush) begin to make their choices. For each day of rush, the event length increases and they become more formal. For instance, if there are 16 sororities on a campus, the first day of rush all the Rushees would attend a short (20–30 minute) event at each sorority house. During the event, the Rushees may get a house tour, watch a skit performed by sorority members, and/or have a snack. The second day of rush, the Rushees select the 12 sororities they would like to return to and the sororities select the women that they would like to invite back to another set of events. If the selection of the Rushees by the sororities matches the selection by the Rushees, that Rushee would attend an event at that house. This process repeats for 4 or 5 days until the final night, which is called Preference Night. The Rushee may attend 1 or 2 house events that night. If a Rushee preferences House A and House A preferences a certain Rushee, we have a match. If the Rushee accepts the bid, she becomes a pledge.

## Fraternity Rush

Fraternity rush is much more informal and relaxed. Generally, the fraternity men will have events each night involving food and entertainment. They may take a group of Rushees bowling or have a volley ball event in their yards. Male Rushees may be given a bid to join the fraternity any time during rush week. At many schools, there are set hours when rush can take place, but the Rushees can go from one house to the next with no set schedule. Alcohol is not permitted during rush.

# Opportunities

RELATIONSHIPS. Probably the greatest advantage for joining a fraternity or sorority is the close relationships that are formed. Many students develop a close bond with friends on the same high school athletic team or youth group. The relationships that develop with a sorority or fraternity exceed the close-knit ties formed in high school and are often life-long.

LEADERSHIP. There are many opportunities available to students who join a fraternity or sorority. Once your son/daughter joins, they have instantly made 20, 30, or 40+ friends who can help them adjust to college and be there for support. Perhaps the greatest opportunity found in Greek life is the opportunity for leadership skills. Each sorority/fraternity has several leadership positions. Some of the positions are very time consuming (president, vice president) while others require less time (activities chair, intramurals chair). Becoming a leader teaches students time management, financial management, project management, public speaking, motivation, delegation, and organizational skills. It is invaluable experience. This leadership experience also opens up many doors for campus leadership positions. On many campuses, Greeks hold the majority of campus-wide leadership positions, thus giving them the opportunity to obtain more leadership skills than non-Greeks.

SCHOLARSHIP is also a focus of sorority or fraternity membership. Each chapter has a Scholarship Chair that monitors the grades of each member. Each chapter has certain grade point standards that all members must maintain. If the standards are not met, members may be placed on probation. The Scholarship Chair is also responsible for conducting programs on study skills and providing incentives for the membership. On many campuses, Greeks form study sessions and review sessions before tests. At many campuses, the sorority/fraternity grade point averages are consistently higher than the all women's/men's grade point averages on campus.

PHILANTHROPY. Greek life also offers opportunities for philanthropic work. Each year, Greek Systems put in several thousand hours of community service work. This teaches Greek members the value of giving of one's self—which will hopefully carry on throughout life. Projects such as building playgrounds, reading to elementary school children and donating blood are popular activities for Greeks.

SOCIAL. The most well-known aspect of Greek life is the social life associated with being Greek. Each campus is different, but approximately 3–4 times per month, a sorority and fraternity will have a party or mixer. Quite often, these mixers are associated with a theme, such as a hay ride, disco party, or other costume party and provide a great opportunity for relaxed, social interaction.

NETWORKING. A less publicized benefit of being Greek is the networking opportunities that take place. Greek students often make connections in the community during their philanthropic projects and through contact with local alumni. Once your son/daughter leaves college, they will have the Greek connections for the rest of their lives. Each sorority/fraternity will most likely have Alumni Chapters in each state. Alumni Chapters consist of men or women in the same sorority that still want to maintain their Greek connections and often assist the local chapters with fundraising, rush and other events.

# Challenges

TIME. While there are many benefits to joining a sorority/fraternity, it is not for everyone. Greek membership takes a substantial time commitment. Depending on how much involvement an individual may want in the chapter, an average of 3–4 hours per week will be spent on Greek-related activities. Some weeks it will be more, such as during Homecoming, and some weeks it will be less, such as finals week. Time management is an important skill learned as a fraternity or sorority member.

MONEY. Being Greek also requires some additional expenses. Each chapter has dues. There are one-time dues for new members and other dues that are paid once or twice a year, such as social dues and chapter dues. Members of fraternities often find that their rent in the fraternity house is less than rent in residence halls, and members of sororities find that their rent is about the same as residence halls.

ALCOHOL. Perhaps the largest challenge associated with being Greek is the perceived alcohol abuse. At most fraternity parties, alcohol is present. However, the national offices of the sororities and fraternities have implemented standards that students must follow for each party. Some standards include: having licensed bartenders, IDs at the door and at the bar, ID bracelets for those over 21 years, busing students to off-campus parties so alcohol-related accidents don't occur, and always having alternative beverages and food available.

One way to investigate what the Greek system is like at your student's school is by calling the Greek Affairs Office. A professional staff member can answer your questions on scholarship and alcohol policies as well as many other areas. You can also ask if any fraternity/sorority has recently been placed on academic or social probation by the college or university. By doing some investigation, you can learn more about Greek life and whether or not it's the right choice for your son or daughter.

# Move-in Day
## Organized Chaos

T he big day has finally arrived! The car is packed, and you and your student are headed to college. Imagine how you will feel: excited, nervous, sad, lost, confused about where to go, anxious. Now, imagine hundreds or thousands of other students and parents feeling the same thing. This is move-in day! Here are some things to expect:

✓ **Hot**—it will most likely be hot. Somehow late August to early September always finds a way to sneak in some really hot days—especially as you will be making dozens of trips from the car into the building. Dress appropriately, take breaks and drink plenty of fluids!

✓ **Crowded**—there will be hundreds or thousands of other people trying to do the same thing you are doing. Parking lots, lobbies, and especially elevators will be especially busy. Plan to arrive as early as possible to avoid the crowds.

✓ **Chaotic**—no one will know exactly what to do. Sure, everyone has a map, but things always look different when the time comes. Look for residence hall staff (often in matching shirts) to give you directions and point you down the correct hallway. It may be a good idea to bring a hand cart or luggage cart to make the trips to the room a little easier!

✓ **Little parking**—college campuses never have enough parking, especially when hundreds of additional cars flood the campus on move-in day. Be prepared to walk. Don't expect to drive right up to the curb and unload your belongings. Some campuses have easier access than others, but expect to see cars everywhere.

✓ **Diversity**. There will be people from small towns, large towns, and other countries. You may see students with purple hair, body piercing, or tattoos. Keep an open mind to the diversity around you.

✓ **Emotions**—think of how you are feeling and multiply that times hundreds or thousands of other parents and students. Emotions run high on move-in day. Dads may be frustrated trying to get the car unloaded quickly, moms may be concerned that something was left at home, students are concerned that they won't fit in, younger siblings may be screaming for attention— imagine this over and over and over. Not to mention—the  sadness, joy and mixed emotions about saying goodbye. Try to stay as calm as possible. Go with the flow.

# So Much to Do, So Little Time

So, you've unpacked the car and you are now sitting in your student's residence hall room. What's next? Here are a few things to take care of:

1. **Let your son/daughter decide how the room will be arranged.** Offer to help unpack suitcases and boxes, but let your student and his/her roommate be in control. This is especially crucial if the roommate is already here and they are negotiating space. Your student will let you know the amount of involvement they want you to have in unpacking their room. Some students will want you to stay until the last picture is put on the wall. Other students will want your help carrying their belongings to their room, and they will want you to leave. You may want to ask about these expectations ahead of time so you are not disappointed if you are asked to leave earlier than you had planned. Incidentally, bring a phillips and flat head screwdriver and a hammer with you just in case!

2. **Meet the roommate and his/her parents—if possible.** Establishing a relationship (even if it's short) with the roommate and his/her family will give you an idea of what to expect. You'll get a chance to learn about their family and have some other people to go through this experience with. It's a good idea to exchange phone numbers so you can reach the student and/or parent over breaks or in case of emergency.

3. **Keep a list** of everything that was left at home or that you are just now finding out you need (extension cords, light bulbs, waste basket). Make a trip to a grocery store and a discount store to pick up last minute items for your student.

4. **Miscellaneous.** If you plan on renting a refrigerator, buying a loft or opening a bank account—take care of it today.

# Bon Voyage: Saying Goodbye

You've unpacked their belongings, taken them to the store and now the inevitable is at hand. How do you say goodbye? Many colleges will have activities planned so students will have something to do their first night and not think about being homesick. If this is the case for you, talk to your student about when they would like you to leave. They may want some time to shower and change clothes for their first college activity. You don't want to crowd them and make them feel rushed.

If there is nothing planned the first night, take your student out to dinner. This will give you a chance to say goodbye and spend some time alone as a family. Even if you think you know your son/daughter really well, you may not be able to predict how they will react to your leaving. The toughest guy may start to cry or the shy wallflower may give you a quick hug and run up to join her roommate. Be prepared for anything.

If you think it will be an emotional goodbye, try to make it quick. The longer you stand at the door saying goodbye, the more your student will think about what is happening. If you start to cry, don't feel bad, because you won't be alone. There will be many other parents with tear-filled eyes trying to say goodbye to their children.

# The Drive Home

Take advantage of the drive home to reminisce about your son/daughter. Think of the fun you've had as a family. Remember his/her first day of kindergarten. Laugh. Cry. Do whatever you need to do. In a way, you have experienced a loss. You still have a son or daughter, but they have left home and have begun their life as an adult. Ask yourself if your son/daughter is happy. If the answer is yes, than you may wish to take the attitude, "If my son/daughter is happy, then I can be happy."

You will begin to relate to your son/daughter in a different way. You will begin to form a new relationship. You can learn more about how to manage this new relationship in "Parenting From Afar" in Chapter 8.

# Your First Visit

The first time the family goes to visit your college student can be challenging. Both you and your student have certain expectations about the visit. Here are the most important things to consider as you plan your visit:

1. **Always let him/her know you are coming.** Never come unannounced. Your student may have big plans or a big test to study for. And if you come unannounced, his/her room will most certainly be messy!

2. **Plan something to do during your visit.** Whether it's touring the town, going out to dinner or taking a campus tour—always have something planned during your visit. If you don't, you will spend a lot of time sitting in your son's or daughter's room.

3. **Plan to take your student shopping.** College students are always eager to get "freebies" when mom and dad come to visit. Take them to the grocery store or to a discount store so they can stash up on some supplies.

4. **If you have family or personal issues to discuss**, never discuss them in front of a roommate. There are some things your student will want kept private.

5. **If you will be staying overnight, make reservations in advance.** Many college towns have a limited number of hotel rooms. It would not be fun to be caught 400 miles from home with no place to stay. Parents/guardians should not plan to stay overnight in their student's residence hall room. It is unfair to the roommates and can be awkward for everyone.

6. **Never come empty-handed.** Whether its food, shampoo, money, a pair of socks or a new outfit—bring them something from home! College students love to brag to their friends about what their parent(s) brought them during their visit. Even if it's a batch of cookies—your son or daughter will be proud to say the cookies are from home!

# On Their Own
## Parenting from Afar

**L**etting go of your college bound young adult elicits a complex blend of emotions including relief, pride, and panic. It's nice to have fewer dirty socks to pick up off the floor. You're proud to see your own flesh and blood take the next big step toward maturity and financial independence. And you worry whether your son or daughter will be able to make it unscathed. You hope you've laid a solid foundation for your student, but it's hard not to feel a little helpless at this stage. At times, it feels like (s)he's living on the dark side of the moon.

## Young Adult Development

Your role as a parent should complement what your son or daughter is going through. While no two college students are identical, all young men and women must go through a transition from child to adult. This transition consists of managing two complex and inter-related tasks: forming an identity and forming relationships. They start these "developmental tasks" long before they reach college, but they haven't finished them yet.

Identity formation or "Who am I?" has to do with such weighty issues as deciding on a philosophy of life, religious convictions, and political beliefs. Do I share my parents' view of the world and will I practice their religious traditions or lack thereof? What kind of a citizen and voter will I be? Identity formation also has to do with deciding what is interesting and important. What will I major in, and what career will I pursue? What activities and hobbies most bring me satisfaction? Establishing an identiy also deals with discovering the extent and limits of one's abilities. Can I succeed in college? Get into medical school? Meet or surpass an employer's expectations?

Intimacy or "Who will I care about?" refers to the capacity to form significant relationships. Who do I play with? Who do I work with and study with? Who are friends, and who are merely acquaintances? Can I "fit in" with a group of people? Whom will I love?

The thing about these big questions is that you no longer have a huge amount of influence on how your children answer them. You've had your say for 18 years, and you hope you have laid a firm foundation for a healthy and productive life. But these are questions no person can answer for another. Your sons or daughters must finally decide for themselves. Students need considerable freedom in order to grow into independent, self sufficient adults. During this process, they will make mistakes, but there is no other way for them to become adults themselves. That is the hardest part about parenting a college student. This may be why many of us are convinced that mental illness is genetic: we inherit it from our children!

## The Parent's Role

Letting go doesn't mean you are completely helpless or devoid of influence. It does mean that your influence is of a different sort than when your children were younger. During earlier stages of your children's development you instructed, directed, and protected. Now you must operate more as a consultant, friend, and mentor. The relationship started out vertical. You were the adult, and you had the power. You're rapidly moving toward a more horizontal, egalitarian relationship. Both sides should be considered adult. Just what can you do to effectively parent a college student? We believe there are three things:

1. You can support and encourage.
2. You can advise and inform.
3. You can set limits.

These three actions are in descending order of power. It will be easier for you to encourage than to advise, and easier to advise than to limit.

Your ability to set limits is drastically different than when your child was a toddler, and it's substantially different than when (s)he was in high school. If your college student lives on campus, you will not be able to regulate his comings and goings, when or even whether he goes to bed. You cannot control her study habits or restrict her friendships. Different colleges exercise varying degrees of control. Military colleges and a few church-related schools are very structured and have many rules and regulations. Most colleges, however, accord their students a degree of freedom that may exceed the maturity of 18- and 19-year-olds: no curfews and no study hours. Most students learn quickly enough that they cannot pass without sleep or study.

Another factor which limits your ability to influence your son or daughter is the Federal Education Rights and Privacy Act. Also known as the Buckley Amendment, this legislation can make it difficult to know just what your son or daughter is up to. Unless students are under eighteen, it is against the law for any university to disclose information about them to anyone—including their family. Unless your son or daughter waives their right to privacy, the college cannot tell you their grades, their medical problems, or their disciplinary history. Your student could attend no classes, pass no courses, and live in the waiting room outside the dean's office because of repeated violations of campus codes of conduct: and you would STILL not be informed unless the student agreed to a release of information. There could be a sexually transmitted disease, an unwanted pregnancy, and substance abuse. You'd still be in the dark.

There is a solution to this problem on some campuses, and that is a waiver of privacy. Some schools require the submission of a form, others, a letter from the student which states precisely which privacy rights are waived. Other schools will not allow their students to waive their rights to privacy. They leave it up to the student to keep the parents informed. You should discuss this issue well before school starts. Many parents believe they have a "parental" right to know grades and disciplinary violations, and you may want to request that your son or daughter grant you this right if the school permits it. If your student asks the school to send grades to the family home address, you'll get the grade report at the end of every semester. Regarding medical and mental health matters, many student affairs professionals recommend that you respect your student's privacy, but encourage him or her to keep you informed. Obviously, there can be tricky situations when a young adult has a history of substance abuse, depression, or an eating disorder. In these situations, we recommend a consultation with a mental health professional who specializes in these areas to advise you on the privacy issue. Sometimes privacy is in order. Sometimes family involvement is. Even if students sign a waiver with the university, counseling centers and health centers will probably require students to sign another form which specifies just what information can be released and to whom and for what period of time.

So far, we've told you how you can't excercise control. Now, we're going to tell you how you can. We're also going to say that you should exercise it judiciously. Micro-managing your son or daughter is not, generally, a very effective means of promoting maturity. Neither is it a formula for promoting familial tranquility.

The most potent source of power most parents have is the purse string. While an occasional student goes to college on some trust fund, and quite a few contribute through work and savings, most traditional age students (those under twenty-five) will depend upon their parents or guardians for partial or complete financial assistance. How you funnel this money to them definitely has an impact. Indeed, it can be tempting to make financial support contingent upon choosing the "right" school and the "right" major, making the "right" grades, and getting the "right" haircut. While it is, after all, your money, we recommend against wielding too heavy a hand. We don't think, however, that college students are necessarily well served by receiving an endless supply of signed blank checks regardless of their behavior.

You have every right to recommend a particular school (usually a parent's alma mater) or category of schools, but we advise against insisting. The same is true with the selection of a major. We have, in fact, seen many college students flunk themselves out of their parents' choice of school or major rather than confront Mom and Dad head on. When they pursue their own dream they manage to perform quite adequately.

Whatever expectations you have, we recommend that you be up front about them. "This is how much money we will devote toward your education. After it's gone, it's up to you. We have confidence that you'll make the most of it." Or, "We will back you financially as long as you're making reasonable progress toward graduation." Or, "You have been dropped from school twice, once for academic reasons, once for social misconduct. After your next penalty, we are not willing to invest further money in an education that you seem less interested in than we are."

Should you make financial support contingent upon making good grades? In general, probably not. You should always factor in your child's abilities and situation. How competitive is the school? What is the average grade point of last year's freshman class? Of graduating seniors? What is the major in question? Typically, the academic competition is tougher and it's harder to make A's in theoretical physics or pre-med than recreational administration. Typically, college grades are lower than high school grades. Be wary of comparing your collegiate experience to that of your son's or daughter's. While some comparisons hold up, others don't. Did you attend a different college? Select a different major? If you did not attend college yourself, you should bear in mind that college is more demanding than high school, and the competition is stiffer. Punishing your child because (s)he doesn't make all A's is very likely inappropriate and ineffective as well.

Moving up from control to advice, you will probably find that your student may not be substantially more interested in your advice than in your restrictions. Recommendations and suggestions always work best when they're requested. If you have cultivated a collaborative relationship with your son or daughter, they may well ask for your advice. It is even possible that they will follow it. But remember, advice is advice, not divine revelation, nor royal edict. Be prepared to have your son or daughter make different choices than you would. And try your best not to say "I told you so" whenever the overpowering urge to do so strikes—which it almost invariably will.

Finally, support and encouragement are actions which your child WILL hear and appreciate. And speaking of hearing, one of the best ways to demonstrate your support is by listening. One mother's parting words were: "If you need to call us, call us. No matter if it's three o'clock in the morning. I don't care if you're flunking out or if you're in jail: we love you and will be there for you." This was the one message this student remembers above all the others. It speaks volumes about good parenting, and it is available to every parent of every college student.

# Maintaining Contact

Keeping contact with your son or daughter at college is something you will want to talk about before they leave. Whatever your means of communication, it is wise to set some guidelines and expectations.

## Telephone

If your family stays in touch by telephone, talk about the time(s) of day and day(s) of the week that are most convenient. Some families keep a regular calling schedule of Sunday evenings. That way a schedule is set and everyone knows the expectations. Other families choose not to have a set schedule and call each other whenever the need arises. Either way, decide ahead of time who will pay for the call. Many college students have a long-distance card that the parents pay for and the student can only use to call home. Long-distance carriers also offer 1-888 numbers. The 1-888 numbers are similar to 1-800 numbers in that your student can call your 1-888 home number from any telephone without using a long-distance card. You should also consider that calling your student more than once or twice a week can be disruptive to study schedules and can discourage independence and self-reliance.

## Writing Letters

Writing letters seems to be less popular each year with college students. Many students don't have the time to sit down and write a letter, address the envelope, find a stamp and then make sure it gets mailed. However, just because your student doesn't write you doesn't mean they don't want mail FROM you. College students LOVE mail from home. Even if it's just a quick note to say hello or a picture from a family event, send them something! It is also nice for students to get "Care Packages" from home that could include cookies, shampoo, clippings from the local paper, a new shirt or whatever your son/daughter would like. Getting anything from home is always a welcome surprise! Dollar stores are great for simple and inexpensive items.

 Most campuses either have mailboxes in the residence halls or have a central campus postoffice box system for all students to use. The information you receive from housing/residence life should tell you how your son/daughter can receive mail as well as the proper way to address the envelope.

## Electronic Mail

If you can manage it, we strongly recommend that you get the capacity to use e-mail if you don't already have it. Communication on most colleges would grind to a halt without electronic mail. Your sons and daughters are on a steady diet of e-mail from professors, campus organizations, and friends who attend other colleges. The surest way to stay in contact for most parents of college students is via cyberspace.

Encouragement may be even more important when your college student stumbles—and, at some point, (s)he almost certainly will. Indeed, if students never experience any setbacks or failures, they probably aren't taking on enough challenges. The first C or F, dropping a class, not getting a bid from the preferred fraternity or sorority, losing an election, losing a wallet or book bag, and losing the love of one's life can feel devastating. Knowing that the family still cares can provide a real emotional lift.

## Letting Go

There is one other thing you can do, and it is probably the most difficult: you can let go. Ultimately, your son or daughter must succeed or fail on their own. They must learn to take action and live with the consequences. They must become responsible for their own behavior. We spoke to a number of students about what THEY wanted from their parents. The majority wanted less parental interference in their lives. One young woman, who has matured into a model student and citizen, reported that her parents seemed to second guess every decision she made her first two years in school. They wanted to know every grade on every quiz and every piece of homework. They were thrown into a panic when she decided to change majors. They couldn't understand why she wanted to join the co-operative plan when it meant another year in school. Neither of her parents had gone to college and didn't appreciate the typical drop in grades that occurs in a large state university. They didn't understand that a 55 out of a 100 might turn out to be an A after the curve in some classes. They didn't realize that the majority of college students change majors at least once. And they didn't fully comprehend the value that career-related work experience adds to a co-op student's degree. Once Mom and Dad began to cut this student a little slack, the whole family felt a lot better.

# Specific Issues

HOMESICKNESS. It is normal for some students to go through their own period of letting go. Leaving home, family, and friends behind is an adjustment. Some students run up a long distance phone bill that will rival their tuition and fees. A few plead for permission to withdraw from school. This period typically passes once the student emotionally digests that adulthood is a requirement, not an option. If your son or daughter continues to languish away from home, a few visits to the counseling center will likely get them over the hump. If homesickness remains acute after the first term, something is amiss, and a visit to the counseling center is a must.

FRIENDS. Your son or daughter will form new relationships. Not all of them may be to your liking. Remember, learning who one's friends are is part of becoming an adult. Friends are also a big factor in determining the quality of your child's education. If your son or daughter spends time with responsible, well-rounded students, (s)he also will tend to behave more maturely.

ROOMMATES. Whether they choose their roommates or take pot luck, there will likely be adjustments both sides must make. That is, in fact, one of the benefits of living in a residence hall. One is challenged to create a workable relationship within the confines of a space not much larger than a bath tub. This means learning to compromise. It also means learning to stick up for one's rights. Both are useful lessons to learn.

Generally, departments of housing permit students to change roommates subject to the availability of space. (In some schools, there is a waiting period to discourage capricious roommate changing.) Serious Suzy can move in with Studious Stella and won't have to put up with Party Girl Patty and her late night friends. Residence hall staffers are quite accustomed to roommate conflicts and are trained to help negotiate realistic agreements. Many residence halls maintain quiet hours (often resident determined) to promote study and sleep and a measure of civility.

ROMANCE. When society throws together thousands of young men and women who share similar interests, it's not surprising that relationships flourish. Again, you have little choice over who your son or daughter will spend time with, but it's likely they will start spending time with someone. Bear in mind also that the ups and downs of a 25-week romance tend to be more volatile than those which occur after 25 years. The end of a passionate romance might not mean much in the ultimate scheme of things, but it can be all-consuming in the short run. Students have missed deadlines, bombed on tests, and flunked important classes—all because of unrequited love. Remind yourself that this too shall pass. It is unlikely that they will be interested in this piece of information. What they most want—and need—to know is that it's OK to grieve the loss of a love.

ACADEMICS. Surveys consistently indicate that freshmen expect to make grades as good or better than those they got in high school. The facts are that they probably won't. In high school, most studied fewer than five hours a week and still did well enough to get into college. It takes most of them a while to figure out that they have to study a lot more and a lot more effectively to succeed at the next level. The competition is probably stiffer. The faculty's expectations are higher, and the material is more complex. There may be a grading curve which guarantees that not everybody will make A's & B's. And students spend less time in class and more time in the library, the lab, and doing homework. At least, they're supposed to be doing homework. Since not all professors grade the homework, students may be tempted to skip much of it.

Advisement is an important part of the academic picture. The quality of advisement varies widely from school to school and within schools. Many colleges and universities use a faculty advisement system. Each faculty member is assigned a set number of advisees. Some departments designate a particular faculty member or members to do the advising. In other cases, universities or departments within them employ full-time advisors whose only role is to guide students through the right courses toward their degrees. Full-time non-faculty advisors tend to know the catalog very well and have a clear picture of just what courses are required to get through the various degree plans. Faculty are better at guiding students through that faculty member's major. They also typically have solid advice about graduate and professional programs that relate to their own specialties. Depending on the professor, some are extremely helpful in promoting good grades, offering career guidance, and serving as a mentor. There are, unfortunately, other professors who regard advisement as a burden to be suffered as little as possible. It is a very useful to have a good working relationship with an advisor. At some large state schools, however, students may not even know who their advisor is. Ask your student about the quality of advisement. If it's lame, encourage him or her to request a change of advisors if that's an option.

In most cases, students are accepted into a college because the Admissions Department believes they can succeed. If they're not succeeding, it's probably because they're not working hard enough or effectively enough. After a few stubbed toes, most get the picture. If academic problems persist, a visit to a Learning Resource Center or a Counseling Center can usually help a struggling student get on the right track.

MAJORS & CAREERS. Every year, UCLA's Alexander Astin conducts a survey of hundreds of thousands of college freshmen. For many years now, the survey has indicated that students attend college primarily so they can have better careers and enjoy financial security. Unfortunately, many of them regard a college degree as a silver bullet which will ensure professional success. Many also hold idealized versions of the careers that they plan. So it's not surprising that over half of all college students make at least one change of major. This is not necessarily a bad thing. When you consider the complexity of the modern world of work, it's rather unrealistic to expect an 18-year old to have it all figured out. They need some time (a year or two) and experience (some relevant classes and internships) to make sense out of their plans. After all, most of us made a few false starts before we discovered what would work.

Most colleges and universities have agencies to help students find a suitable major and identify a career which matches their interests and abilities. There is also assistance available for students to start networking, write resumes, and interview effectively. There will likely be an office to help with internships and co-op jobs as well. There is only one thing: these counselors, advisors, and placement officials can't help students who don't use their services. We've already implied that it is no sin for freshmen to be uncertain regarding their futures. The sin is in waiting passively for the answers to be revealed. Career counseling is expensive when you find a professional out of the yellow pages. At most colleges and universities, it's free. Encourage your son or daughter to take advantage of these services and to do so before they're about to graduate. For more information, see Chapter 10 on Career Planning.

# Choices

Many parents are worried about some important choices that college students must make. Now that they are relatively free of adult supervision, what will they decide about alcohol, drugs, and sex? First, we think you should be aware of the national trends for all college students. Statistics don't guarantee what your individual son or daughter will do, but they do give you a general idea of what to expect.

ALCOHOL & DRUGS. The most popular campus drug is still alcohol, and that is true by a wide margin. The Harvard School of Public Health reported in 1995 that a significant number of undergraduate students engaged in binge drinking. (Binge drinking was defined as "five or more drinks in a row one or more times during a two week period for men, and four or more drinks in a row one or more times during the same period for women.") The rates of binging varied widely from school to school—from 1% to 70%. "At nearly one-third of the schools, more than half of the responding students were binge drinkers." At these schools, nearly one-third of the students were classified as frequent bingers. "Fully 84% of all students drank during the school year. Nearly half (44% were binge drinkers, and 19% were frequent binge drinkers) binged three or more times in the past two weeks." This last set of statistics refers to the entire sample drawn to represent the entire American college student population. In other words, the vast majority of college students drink, at least occasionally; almost half sometimes drink to excess, and one in five drinks excessively on a regular basis.

The news about other drugs is somewhat less alarming. The same Harvard study reported that 22% had smoked cigarettes within the last 30 days. Thirteen percent had smoked marijuana during that same period. In a nationwide longitudinal study of drug use among full-time college students conducted by the National Institute on Drug Abuse it was found that most drug use gradually went down after 1980. In recent years, however, the use of illicit drugs has begun to increase again. In 1995, 31.2 percent of college students used marijuana at least once. For other drugs the incidence was: LSD—6.9%, cocaine—3.6%, crack cocaine—1.1%.

Sex. According to the Centers for Disease Control and Prevention, before age 17, about two thirds of the men and a little over half the women have already become sexually active. In "Sex and America's Teenagers," the Alan Guttmacher Institute reports that 73% of males and 56% of females have had sex by age 18. The American College Health Association Journal notes that by the time they are college seniors, 90% of all students have had intercourse. One in eight college students will contract a sexually transmitted disease. The most common STD on college campuses is Chlamydia, a bacterial infection. Both men and women are susceptible to it. In men, Chlamydia is the leading cause of urinary tract infection, as well as a common cause of testicular inflammation. In women, there is more concern, because there often are no early symptoms, but if left untreated, complications can lead to serious problems including infertility. Four-fifths of sexually active teenagers say that they regularly use contraceptives. Only 40%, however, seek medical contraceptive services within a year after beginning intercourse. While many factors determine the sexual practices of your son or daughter, there clearly is a risk of pregnancy or contracting a sexually transmitted disease.

When you consider the high incidence of binge drinking cited earlier, it is not surprising that unwanted or unprotected sex occurs: the one often precedes the other. The vast majority of acquaintance rapes involve alcohol. If your daughter drinks excessively on dates and at parties, she places herself at risk. If your son does, his chances of appearing before the college judiciary on a date-rape charge go up dramatically. Arguably the most important determinant of responsible sexual behavior among college students is the responsible use of alcohol. The first six weeks of college are particularly crucial in this regard: It's a new environment. There is excitement and anxiety. There is peer pressure. Students are supervised much less closely than when they lived at home.

As if you didn't have enough to worry about, the past few years have seen the introduction of Rohypnol as an aid to sexual "seduction." Seduction doesn't really accurately describe what this prescription sedative accomplishes when dissolved in a target's drink. Tasteless and odorless, the drug quickly induces a state of intoxication which usually renders the victim comatose. The victim is at the mercy of the unscrupulous person who spiked the drink, as well as anyone else in the vicinity. The victim may have little or no memory of what transpired.

Students, most likely men, should know they are treading on extremely dangerous ground if they use this drug to gain sexual gratification. Rohypnol, or The Date-Rape Drug, is illegal to possess in the United States. If someone is convicted of using it to perpetrate a sexual crime, the penalties are much more severe than for mere possession. Women should know that Rohypnol-induced sexual assaults do occur. Your daughter should be wary of who is providing her drinks.

It's a good idea for women to go to parties with a buddy system until they know which parties and crowds are trustworthy.

If a student believes she was the victim of a Rohypnol-induced sexual assault, she should talk to the police as quickly as possible. She can be tested for the presence of the drug in her bloodstream for up to 48 hours from the time the substance was ingested. Additionally, it is wise for her to get some counseling. Students who seek counseling after such incidents are more likely to recover quickly than those who don't.

COLLEGE STUDENTS CHANGE. Going to college means your sons and daughters will change schools and teachers. In many cases they will also change friends. They may change where they sleep and eat, in some cases moving across the state, in others, across the country. New expectations are placed upon them. So it's not surprising that they, themselves, undergo change. Some of the changes are peripheral, but they may be expressions of more profound changes. Junior becomes Frank. Chrissy becomes Christine. High school slang and colloquialisms fade from use and are replaced by those that prevail in college, or, at any rate, at that particular college. New interests may flourish. Some of them will endure as lifelong avocations. Others may develop into newfound careers. Still others virtually explode onto the scene, then are forgotten completely a short while later.

RELIGION. Among the changes which can be particularly threatening to parents are those involving religious convictions. Agnostic parents may find their child has been born again. Devout Christians may discover their child has profound doubts about the validity of any religion. Christians may explore Judaism or Islam. Protestants might become fascinated with Catholicism. Many schools are host to large contingents of international students, some of whom practice Islam, Buddhism, or Hinduism. These religious traditions that might be new to your son or daughter may inspire newfound devotion. Sometimes these changes pass as quickly as they came. But not always. We would add that an exploration of these issues can also lead to a reaffirmation of one's faith.

CULTS. Perhaps even more frightening, there are a variety of cults whose disciples are only too happy to enlist your student into their cause. While there is no litmus test that infallibly identifies adherents to cults, dramatic changes in habits and life style can be tip-offs. Has your student donated all his school money to the new-found cause? Does (s)he completely abandon classes and books and devote all time and energy to proselytizing and fund raising? A useful resource is The American Family Foundation. Founded in 1979, they study cult behavior, conduct educational programs, and help families and ex-cult members. Their web site is http://www.csj.org. The phone number is (212) 533-5420.

VISITS HOME. Two events—winter break and spring break—may rudely confront you with the extent to which your son or daughter has changed. Winter break is significant because it may be the first time your child has visited since you dropped him or her off on campus. Even if they've visited earlier, this time they're around long enough for the changes to produce conflict. Chances are, they've been used to coming and going according to their own whims and whatever constraints their academics impose. Their sleeping habits may be different. They're not used to a curfew, and they may interpret your requests for an itinerary as heavy handed. They may want to spend more time with old high school pals than with family.

Try to remember what you felt like when you first returned home. Make clear that you're not policing their behavior, but you're counting on a little courtesy from your favorite visitors. Of course, they want to see old friends and compare notes with them. But no more than you are eager to visit with them, so why not plan some family time interspersed with free time,

time with friends, and time to sleep. College students seem to have a boundless capacity for sleep when they get back to their own beds. Unfortunately, it is often during day time hours! And, speaking of night time, their bed times may be quite different than yours. If they don't already have their own house key, they probably should be given one.

Don't be completely shocked by the presence of tattoos, piercings, novel haircuts, or hair colors. These are ways late adolescents explore their identities.

Spring break is important because it may mean you won't get to see them at all. There may also be issues of financing this venture as well as concerns about the safety of your son or daughter partying with several thousand other maturity challenged, judgment impaired collegians. Be clear up front about how far you're willing to support a spring vacation. We think it's not unreasonable to know with whom they'll travel, where they're headed, and when they'll return. And you'd like to know when they get back (preferably in one piece) on campus. Happily, there are some alternative spring break opportunities promoted by a number of colleges: archeological digs, missions of mercy to third world countries, and construction projects in American locations which have suffered natural disasters. These spring breaks may well prove more memorable than endless cruising and bottomless kegs.

# First Six Weeks

You'll probably worry the most about your student during the first few weeks (s)he's away at school. You're still adjusting to the new relationship with your collegian as it unfolds. The first six weeks are, in fact, regarded by college administrators as particularly critical for students. They're still forming many new relationships with relative strangers. They're adjusting to a more challenging academic environment. They're trying on new behaviors and new perspectives. They're on their own.

# First Six Weeks

**Peer Pressure to drink excessively &
to have unwanted/unprotected sex**

| Greek Rush | Roommate | Not | | | |
| Homesick | problems | "fitting in" | | 1st Bad Grades | |
| Week 1 | 2 | 3 | 4 | 5 | 6 |

# First Year

After the first six weeks, college administrators
regard the first year as the next most critical period
of time in a student's success.

| | | | | | | Midterms | | | |
| | | | | | | Spring Break | | | |
| First Six | | Visit Home | | | | Careers/ | | Finals | |
| Weeks | | | Finals | | | Majors? | Registration | | |
| Month 1 | 2 | 3 | 4 | 5 | 6 | 7 | 8 | 9 | 10 |

# Signs of Trouble

Dear Mom & Dad,

Well, the leg is almost healed now, and I'm feeling much better. But I haven't written for awhile so I'd better catch you up on news.

Oh yes, you're wondering about the leg. I broke it jumping out of the window when the dorm caught on fire. Unfortunately, I lost all my stuff and had no place to stay. But just like you always told me: "Behind every cloud there's a silver lining." That's when I met Frank. He was so sweet and said I could move in with him until things settled down for me, which they finally have. Of course I'll be staying with Frank anyway now that we're going to be parents ourselves. Won't the Jones next door be positively green with envy when they find out you'll be the first grandparents on the block?

Yes, I'm in love, and I'm so eager for you to meet him. Frank is so special that I know you're going to adore him even though his religious and political views are so different from yours. Also Daddy, do you think maybe you could help him get a job with the bank? Frank's had some trouble getting work the last year or so, but then his parole officer hasn't helped at all.

Love,
Snookums

P.S.: OK, don't panic. There was no fire. I didn't break my leg. There's no Frank. I'm not pregnant. I did get an F in Chemistry though, and I just wanted you to keep things in perspective.

Your role as a parent is different with a college student away at a university than it is with a younger child who lives at home. For one thing, it is more difficult to know what difficulties your son or daughter might be facing. There are, however, signs of trouble. You should not watch for them obsessively, but you certainly should not ignore them when they become obvious. What are they?

GRADES. Bad grades are a problem because a student won't get a degree without a certain minimum grade point average (GPA). Mediocre grades CAN be a problem if a student aspires to post graduate education. Typically, graduate and professional schools won't accept students with a transcript dominated by C's. The top programs require mostly A's. We anticipate that advanced degrees will grow in importance in the 21st century. So, good grades are important. Outstanding grades are better.

It is most possible for students to succeed in their careers and in life with marginal grades. They will not, however, do it as brain surgeons or corporate lawyers. They simply won't be able to get the training. There is, in fact, very little correlation between grades and long term success. There are many factors—motivation, character, and a variety of people skills—that can take a person a very long way. Daniel Goleman's *Emotional Intelligence*, available at most bookstores, speaks eloquently on this topic.

In any event, parents should not panic with the first C or even a D or an F. After an easy ride through high school, many a college student has had a wake up call in the form of a disastrous exam or even a failed course or more. The question you must ask is "why?" There are basically two reasons: Skills and Ability or *can't* and *won't*. It is generally, but not invariably, possible for the student to change either one.

ABILITY. There are several reasons why a student is unable to perform adequately at the college level. Let's take a look at the principle ones:

LEARNING DISABILITIES. A learning disability is often difficult to diagnose. Faculty sometimes are resistant to the very idea of such difficulties. The symptoms which suggest an LD can also point to poor motivation or lower scholastic aptitude. It takes a specially trained diagnostician to identify the legitimate LD from the pretender. Federal law (The Americans with Disabilities Act) requires schools to reasonably accommodate students with disabilities, including learning disabilities. Talk with the administrator who is responsible for students with disabilities. (S)He will know where you can get an accurate evaluation. The LD student must identify as such to the college. Further, colleges typically require verification of a learning disability by a licensed professional before they can provide assistance to the student. Assistance could be in the form of increased time in which to take tests, taking tests in a distraction free environment, or having a reader or note taker.

Symptoms which suggest the possibility of a learning disability include:

✓ Diligent study for long hours with poor results on tests

✓ Reading and rereading textbook material without being sure of what was read

✓ Consistently being the last person to finish tests

✓ Difficulties with memorization

✓ Reversing letters and numerals

POOR PREPARATION. If your student did not take many college prep courses and is competing with students who have, (s)he will probably struggle for a while until (s)he catches up. Even among students who have taken the same course work, it isn't necessarily really the same. High schools vary dramatically in terms of their quality and the height of their expectations for their students. An A from a top flight prep school is different from an A in a less challenging school. If your student starts out behind, (s)he should be encouraged to take fewer hours per term, to take more basic courses, and to get plenty of tutoring. It may even be appropriate to transfer to a two-year college until the basics are mastered. So, how many hours should students carry during their first term? The typical load in most schools is around 15 hours. If your student seems to be at a competitive disadvantage, 12 hours may be in order during the very first school term. Alternatively, (s)he can register for 15 or more hours, then drop a class if disaster looms ahead. The down side of a reduced course load is that it will take longer to graduate, and that can cost money. If you have questions, your student's academic advisor should have a good feel for what is a reasonable load at your particular school.

ANXIETY. Emotional states DO impact performance. Test anxiety can hurt grades. Moreover, once a student has bombed on a test, (s)he will tend to be anxious on the next test. Each successive failure due to anxiety fuels the student's anxiety, and it is possible for him or her to spiral downward into a series of panic attacks and a loss of confidence. Generally speaking, this condition can be treated in the counseling center in a relatively limited amount of time. Typically, students are taught to relax while performing under pressure and taught to think constructively instead of catastrophically in test-taking situations.

POOR STUDY SKILLS. If students did well in high school with little effort, there is a good chance that they did not acquire effective study skills. Reading a chemistry text is different than reading literature which is different than reading the sports page. There is an art to taking good notes, and most students don't practice effective review until poor grades force them to do so. Many freshmen do not manage their time well. An inexpensive planner

can be a useful gift for a disorganized student.
Obviously, a planner doesn't work very well if
your student never opens it. A learning resource
center or a counseling center can provide effective
assistance. In many schools, there are study skills
courses which can be taken. Some schools require freshmen to
take a University 101 or Freshman Success class. Many others,
but not all, make it optional. We believe it is usually an excellent
investment of a student's time and energy. Also, see the More to
Read Appendix for books on Study Skills and Freshman Success.

INSUFFICIENT ABILITY. While most students who attend college
have the ability to do the work if they apply themselves, some
do not. Nor do all students who aspire to be neurosurgeons
or rocket scientists have the ability to master organic chemistry
or quantum mechanics. SAT scores and College Board scores
do NOT measure pure intelligence. They measure readiness to
perform in an academic setting, which is certainly related to
intelligence. There is, in fact, NO measure of pure intelligence.
The current thinking is that there are a variety of intelligences,
and they don't all help out equally in the classroom. On the other
hand, all things being equal (which they never are) students with
high SAT's make better grades than students with low SAT's.
There are, however, so many confounding variables that sometimes students with low scores excel. And some students with
scores in the stratosphere make grades below C level.

MOTIVATION. It has been our experience that the most likely
reason for poor grades is poor effort. The causes of poor effort
can vary.

NOT USED TO HARD WORK. Bright students who weren't challenged in high school are not used to the amount of effort it takes
to negotiate a rigorous college curriculum. According to
Alexander Astin's annual CIRP survey of college freshmen, the
majority are used to studying fewer than five hours per week.
For many, it takes a few academic stubbed toes to realize that

there is no easy road to good grades. You might liken a college freshman to an aspiring marathoner who is woefully out of shape. It takes long hours of running to develop the endurance it takes to run 26 miles. It also takes many freshmen a term or two to get used to the idea of working hard on a regular basis, to realize that they can't do it all the last week of the semester, and that cramming will take them only so far.

DISTRACTIONS. Most freshmen don't lack for alternatives to studying. Some lose themselves in television and video games. A few play poker or bridge around the clock. Greek life, which develops scholarship as well as leadership for some, promotes anti-intellectualism and slackerdom in others. Nor are the only party animals those in Greek houses. If your son or daughter is working more than ten hours a week, that can cut into school time. What it boils down to is that your son or daughter may not yet possess the inner character required to cope with the relative lack of structure in most college settings.

Some universities offer residential plans for freshmen which include tutoring, mentoring, and study hours. There are learning resource centers and counseling centers which can help students maintain a balance between school and other activities. Freshmen Seminars, mentioned above, can also assist students in staying productive scholastically.

POOR ORGANIZATIONAL SKILLS. We still encounter college students without a watch, much less a planner. Many have never had to juggle the number of activities available to the typical college student. Learning resource centers and Freshman Seminars can help students to develop effective organizational skills. The gift of a planner or "Day Timer" can be extremely helpful—if it is used.

WRONG MAJOR/WRONG SCHOOL. Over the years, we have developed a great appreciation for ambitious, conscientious students. They have to work hard, but their professional opportunities in the high tech world of the 21st Century seem limitless. We have also known more than a few who had very little business studying what they were studying. They just didn't have the matching aptitude or interest. In some cases, they wanted to please their parents. In other cases, their parents were pressuring them to pick a particular career bcause it seemed financially promising or it was a family tradition. Whatever the reason, students in the wrong major are much less likely to perform effectively. In some cases, they literally flunk themselves out just to make a point for Mom and Dad. Counseling and career development centers can be enormously effective in assisting students to sort through their options. Career planning courses can also be invaluable.

---

## Bad Grades Action Plan

| DIAGNOSIS | ℞ |
|---|---|
| 1. Find out the cause | 2. Develop a plan |

Is it *can't*?

| | |
|---|---|
| _____ Learning disability? | See Disabilities Coordinator |
| _____ Poor preparation? | Get tutoring & take remedial courses |
| _____ Poor study skills? | Use LRC or Freshman Seminar |
| _____ Inadequate ability? | Transfer to program that matches ability |

Is it *won't*?

| | |
|---|---|
| _____ Not used to hard work? | LRC or Freshman Seminar |
| _____ Distractions? Which ones? | Counseling or LRC |
| _____ Wrong major? | Advisement or Career Services |
| _____ Wrong career? | Career Services or Career Class |

---

CONTACT: TOO MUCH/TOO LITTLE. OVERLY DEPENDENT. If your son or daughter has difficulty breaking away, you'll know it. They call home too often, talk too long, worry too much, and ask for too much advice. They may have difficulty organizing their days or making the most routine decisions. Why is this so? There are several reasons.

Your family could be unusually close—not a bad thing in our highly mobile and transient society. If so, building a new community of support may take a while, and it may take some patience and support on your part. Encourage independence, but allow, within reason, sufficient phone calls and visits to allow time for them to get on their feet.

Your son or daughter could be a slow developer. If (s)he's not especially self sufficient to begin with, adjusting to a new environment can prove to be a formidible task. Again, encourage independence, but provide support. Agree on a plan of contact which will gradually decrease in frequency and scope. Ask your student to visit the counseling center. Counselors are used to working with dependency and know how to set limits for its expression.

Your student could be going through what a lot of other students are going through, but expressing it more vigorously. Everyone falls somewhere on a continuum in their dealings with problems from denial to melodramatic. If your student is on the excitable side, you've probably noticed this before. They have a remarkable capacity for making mountains out of mole hills. Listen to their concerns, but insert the voice of reason in the conversation. Ask them what's the worst thing that could happen? And how likely is that really to occur? If hysterics persist, counseling is a good option.

Little or no contact. She doesn't write. He's never there when you call, nor does he return the messages you leave on his answering machine. You're all for independence, but you'd like some idea that your son or daughter is alive and well. What's going on?

The most likely explanation is that they're caught up in school and campus life, and they also are in the process of breaking away. It is unlikely that every letter any parent writes will get a prompt reply. And college students have a remarkable capacity to stay away from their room until the most ungodly hours, and not always are they up to mischief. The psychological distance will probably run its course, but it may take a few years for it to do so.

There are, however, other possibilities. Students can get caught up in campus life in unhealthy ways. Animal houses do exist on some campuses as do party dorms. In the exhilaration of ongoing party time, it's possible to forget school and Mom and Dad. Occasionally students get sucked into one of the various cults which prey on vulnerable students. While there are typically regulations against it, students do stay overnight in their new sweetheart's room. In some cases, they essentially move in.

It is also possible that your child was not especially close to you BEFORE (s)he left home. If Mom and Dad both have high pressure careers, there isn't much time or energy left for the kids. The psychological distance which troubles you now may have started several years ago.

If contact becomes disturbingly rare, you may wish to contact the Dean of Students. Express your concerns straightforwardly, and ask if your worries are disproportionate to the provocation. Student affairs professionals have a good sense of what fits within the normal range of behavior. They also have the power to call in students to ensure that everything is OK. You may also contact the Resident Advisor (typically a student), the Area Coordinator (typically a full time professional staff member), or the roommate. Don't forget, however, about the Buckley Amendment. Administrators are forbidden by law to reveal information about a student unless that student has granted permission to do so. If you're really worried, you may also wish to contact the roommate's family to find out if they have any sense of what, if anything, is going on. The roommate's parents are in the same boat that you're in. You may get more candor and less public relations from the other parents than from the roommate who doesn't want to "squeal" on another student.

We've stated earlier that it's often a good idea to negotiate a contract for communication with your son or daughter. This may be the time to renegotiate that contract. Sunday evening is phone-in night. If something comes up that prevents them from phoning they are to notify you first. As we have said before, for most students, e-mail is the easiest way to stay in touch. If you send regular e-mails, chances are you'll get at least some of them answered. In this brave new world of new-found independence, don't forget to keep up your side of the bargain, even if their side is lacking. Do send news and clippings from home. Do send cards, small gifts, and goodie packages. In the long run, these efforts usually pay off. If all else fails, one way to get a call home is to send an unsigned check.

FINANCIAL PROBLEMS. The signs are fairly transparent and worrisome: bounced checks, credit card debt, constant complaints about not having enough money. Some students end up working more hours for money than they do for grades, usually to the detriment of their GPA's. What's going on?

First, make sure your student's budget is realistic. If you haven't made out one before, now is the time to do so. You may wish to check with the Dean of Students' Office to get an idea of what it costs most students after tuition and fees. How much do textbooks really cost? Their prices can vary widely depending upon the major and the year in college. The next time you're on campus, you may want to visit the bookstore and see first hand just how much textbooks cost for your student's course schedule.

Once you've determined what a reasonable allowance is, you can figure out a way to provide it. You can also try to find out why your student seems unable to live within that figure. It may simply take a little time for some young men and women to learn to manage their money. Not unlike ourselves, students have an uncanny way of equating wants with needs. Students need food to survive. They do not need to pay for a meal plan they're not using because they eat most meals with their friends in a nearby pizza parlor. Cafeteria food is the source of unending complaints on most college campuses. Our experience is that it is typically more economical and nutritious than the fast food alternatives usually chosen by college students.

There will be a range of incomes and budgets at most universities. If your student is breaking the family bank trying to keep up with Tripp and Muffy who drive Beemers and dine on lobster, you need simply to set some limits. "This is how much we can provide. If you spend your month's budget the first week enjoying the high life, you'd best cultivate a taste for peanut butter and jelly for a while."

If there is too much credit card debt, pull the card, or arrange to lower its limit. Keep going back to a budget that everybody accepts, and stick with it until it works.

WANTS TO TRANSFER. There are a number of reasons why students want to transfer. Some will pass. Some will not. What are they?

One possibility is that your student is homesick or lovesick. (S)He misses family or sweetheart so profoundly that it's difficult to enjoy the campus environment and the opportunities it affords. Usually, but not always, time will solve this problem. If the school genuinely seems to be a good match for your student, strike an agreement: "Stay at this school for the year, after which we'll renegotiate." If the student continues to flounder, encourage the student to seek support and counsel from the counseling center. If that doesn't work, you may wish to request a joint session with the student's counselor to sort things out. Your request will not necessarily be granted, but you should be able to get some sort of consultation over the phone. For those few students who are unable to manage on their own and must transfer, counseling at the new school may be in order. It's also a good idea to negotiate a new understanding. You can stay at home for the rest of this academic year, but you must leave the nest at the beginning of the following fall term.

Another cause of student dissatisfaction can be that your student simply does not fit the prevailing campus culture. A jock will not likely be a happy camper at the University of Chicago. A budding intellectual will feel out of place at a party school. An aspiring general will be much happier at West Point than at Reed College. Granted, not every student can gain admittance into one of the United States military academies, but there are plenty of schools with ROTC programs.

A related, but different issue, is your student's major and career plan. About half of all college students change majors at least once. They may have come for the engineering, but now they want commercial art which High Tech U. does not offer. While capricious changes of career plans should be discouraged, it is normal for change to occur. Provided it is conducted in a thoughtful manner and professional advice and counsel are sought, changing majors can be just what the doctor ordered. Review Chapter 10 on Career Planning, and make sure that your son or daughter is approaching their career planning effectively.

In a similar vein, is the college a good match for the ability of your student? Growth and development occur when students are challenged. Anxiety and defeat occur when they are overwhelmed. And boredom and apathy are likely when things come too easy.

Another question to discuss with the student who is eager to transfer: Are they having difficulty adjusting to this college or to college? If the latter, working for a while can awaken a student's motivation for higher education, particularly since most of their job opportunities will not be near the executive suite. On the other hand, there is in America an unfair bias toward the college educated. For many people, a craft or trade may be more suitable. There are also technical institutes which train people in electronics, computer repair, and mechanics and many other options as well. Isn't what you really want for your son or daughter the training which will maximize their potential? The course of study which will bring them satisfaction and independence?

A final point. Is the school your choice or that of your son or daughter?

## Disciplinary Problems

Your student does not have to be the reincarnation of Bonnie or Clyde to run afoul of university rules and regulations. A school is a community, and there are many ways to betray the community's standards. Some principal standards are academic dishonesty, residential regulations, substance abuse, computing violations, and sexual misconduct.

THE BUCKLEY AMENDMENT. First of all, remember the Buckley Amendment. If your student has not signed a waiver, you will not be notified that your son or daughter is in the university judicial system. Indeed, it is possible for a student to run up a string of violations culminating in expulsion. You learn the truth when your child finally tells you (s)he is coming home.

ACADEMIC DISHONESTY. Because universities are institutions of learning, cheating is regarded as extremely serious on most campuses. Policies vary with the college. In some, cheating means you flunked the test or paper. In others, you flunked the class. In still others, you are suspended or even expelled. Most colleges levy significant penalties, but do not resort to the death penalty— expulsion. In our conversations with students, we have learned that cheating is common in many high schools. This means that your son or daughter may have grown accustomed to a culture of academic dishonesty. They didn't have to cheat in high school, but now they "need" to in order to keep their grades up. Cheating occurs on virtually every campus in the country, but the prevalence of it varies markedly. Peer pressure, the campus culture, and the difficulty of the curriculum can all influence a student's temptation to cheat. What if your student does?

ALCOHOL. A tremendous number of problems arise on most campuses because of alcohol. Vandalism, fighting, accidents, date rape, unprotected sex, and academic problems are all much more likely to occur with excessive amounts of alcohol in one's system. Accordingly, schools try to promote abstinence or at least moderation. As you'll recall from our earlier comments, it doesn't always work out that way.

COMPUTING VIOLATIONS. Because the widespread student use of computers is relatively new, schools are still feeling their way. There are many possible transgressions, however, and some of them are quite serious. Hackers find it very tempting to enter forbidden areas of cyber space. Sometimes, it's simply the thrill of getting through a "locked door." Sometimes, the student wants entry to change grades or financial records. Sometimes, it's a childish desire to crash some system or procedure. Sabotage can cost a university enormous amounts of money.

SEXUAL MISCONDUCT. A recent violation that has drawn a lot of attention from the media is date or acquaintance rape. If a student (usually male) has sex with another (usually female), and the recipient is inebriated, some codes of conduct consider that to be rape. The "victim" was agreeable at the time or passively acquiescent, but could not be regarded as responsible because of her inebriation. If it's your daughter, you may applaud the strict definition of rape. If it's your son, you may fear he's the victim—of political correctness. Whatever, your sons and daughters should know what the campus regulations are.

## Universities Desire Rehabilitation

Universities typically try for rehabilitation after all but the most serious of violations. Campus officials know that eighteen- and nineteen-year-olds are impulsive, subject to peer pressure, and can use bad judgment. If you learn that your student has run afoul of the campus disciplinary process, we hope that you will love and support them. We do not, however, believe they will experience much rehabilitation if your support is in the form of endless litigation. We suppose there are times, when Deans behave like hanging judges, but the vast majority of the campus officials we know want to use discipline to mold students into ethical citizens. If you hire an attorney to get your student off on a legal technicality, what are you teaching him or her about responsibility and integrity?

OK, let's suppose your student is in disciplinary trouble. You want to know if the problems are chronic or severe. If it's not either, modest penalties can have a very salutary effect. If it's either or both, we believe the situation is very serious. You should have a long talk with the Dean of Students and try to work with the university to alter the behavior and attitude of your son or daughter.

MENTAL HEALTH. Young adulthood is a vulnerable time. New challenges typically produce stress which can result in growth, but also in deterioration. College students typically score more abnormally on psychological tests than they will five years later in their lives. Moreover, one of the most serious forms of mental illness—schizophrenia—can emerge at this stage of an individual's life. Directors of college counseling centers report that the incidence of serious emotional problems among their case loads is rising. If your student appears to be having difficulties, what can you do?

First of all, troubled students have rights. They are entitled to an education. A student does not have to be cookie cutter normal in order to earn a degree. Second, most schools provide at least some mental health services. In some cases, it is quite extensive, and it is often free. One of the few bargains left in this world is the free counseling and psychotherapy available on the typical college campus. While, increasingly, the number of free sessions is limited, this is not always so. Even when services are limited, the limitations are often in terms of a set number of individual visits per academic year. The number of group therapy sessions may not be limited. If a student uses their allotment of free therapy judiciously, even moderately disturbed students can manage to get their degree and grow healthier at the same time.

As we have stated before, in addition to the Buckley Amendment, accredited counseling centers observe very stringent codes of ethics. The confidentiality of their case loads is virtually absolute. The only exceptions would be when clients are in danger to themselves or others. If you phone a counseling center to find out about your student's treatment, you will not even be told if (s)he's a client. Often this is an important part of the therapy since it is common for students to be sorting out their independence, their identity, and their relationship with parents.

If there has been a history of emotional difficulties with your student, you may want to speak with one of the college counselors yourself early on. Find out what services are available, how extensive they are, and what cost there is. Sometimes, it is appropriate for the parent(s) to be involved in the therapy, but the therapist will make the final decision on this matter.

Yes, there are pitfalls in college for your student. But life itself is invariably unpredictable and challenging. Your son or daughter probably will suffer a few bumps and bruises, but usually nothing that can't be overcome. Further, there are many campus resources to help students succeed. There is additionally another very important source of help for your student—the one who is reading this book!

# Career
# Planning

In our work on several different college campuses, we have talked with hundreds of parents about a variety of concerns regarding their sons and daughters. We have yet to encounter a parent who was not eager for their child to launch a successful career. Parents are proud when their sons and daughters distinguish themselves professionally. They are also relieved. In an era marked by vocational insecurity (see below), the prospect of your future twenty-somethings roaming your house all night and sleeping all day because they can't find work is not particularly reassuring. But all of us have known young men and women who have had difficult times launching meaningful careers. There is even a term—boomerang children—to describe the college students you mortgaged the farm for: Now they're back home, unable to support themselves, wearing out a path in the carpet between the television and the refrigerator, seemingly on the road to the couch potato hall of fame.

The good news is that your sons and daughters are no less eager than you are to find good careers and financial independence. In fact, Alexander Astin, who coordinates the Cooperative Institutional Research Program at UCLA, reports that the foremost reason contemporary students attend college is to get a good job that pays well.

We have more good news. The college your son or daughter will attend also wants him or her to succeed. Universities want to point to long lines of distinguished graduates who are now business tycoons, Nobel Prize winning scientists, and prominent doctors, lawyers, and educators. College presidents, of course, know that most of their graduates won't be rich and famous, but they want all of them to enjoy successful careers. If too few do, the college will fail. If most find profession and financial independence, raising more funds through the next capital campaign will be a lot easier! The alumni are happy. The state legislature is happy. And you, the parents, are happy.

In order to ensure career success, most colleges and universities provide students with a number of career-related services: counseling centers, career development offices, placement centers, and agencies which help students find internships and co-op jobs. Students can take tests, get counseling, and receive advice. Student professional societies are there for the joining. There are probably free workshops on networking, writing a winning resume, and conducting a killer interview. There is, however, one not-so-small glitch: These services are voluntary, and a tremendous number of students do not use them. Only a small percentage use them all and use them in a timely, effective manner.

Students DO want successful careers. But while they're in college they're mostly concerned with passing courses and having a good time, and not necessarily in that order. It is extremely common for students to make their first visit to their campus career center just before they graduate. Sometimes they wait until after they graduate. At this point, there is obviously no time for planning and strategy, no time for cultivating contacts and acquiring career-related work experience, and no time for developing communication and leadership skills through involvement in campus organizations.

The point we want to make is this: Virtually all college students can graduate poised for career success, but only if they lay the groundwork while they're in college. And nobody makes them lay the groundwork. Faculty, in particular, are often indifferent to their students' vocational concerns. This is not, generally, because professors are heartless eggheads, but because they see their job as teaching and conducting research in their discipline. Advisement is usually about degree plans, not career plans. So, if your sons and daughters want to succeed in the workplace, they need to start laying the foundation for that success as freshmen. They need to complete that foundation, stone by stone, over the next four years.

We have outlined a four-year college plan for career success which is by no means the only way to get there. But it does touch on most of the steps which every student should take to improve their prospects. First, however, you and your son or daughter should know something about the rapidly changing career world that will characterize the 21st century.

## The 21st Century World of Work

The 21st century world of work will be different than the world you faced twenty to thirty years ago. All of the features of the 21st century described below are already in place. Their importance will probably only increase during the years your sons and daughters pursue their careers. Here are seven characteristics of the next century. It is important that your sons and daughters prepare for their world—what lies ahead—rather than your world—what is passing away.

TECHNOLOGY. Computing and telecommunications are the principal drivers here, but global travel also is a factor in creating the world of tomorrow. The significance for tomorrow's job holders is that they must be comfortable with the high technology that already pervades the workplace.

This does not mean that everybody needs to be a computer scientist or computer engineer or even a computer programmer. It does mean that virtually all successful people will be "computer literate." They should know word processing, spread sheets, databases, and presentation software such as Power Point. They should be able to find information on the Internet. They will use e-mail more than the U.S. Postal Service.

More schools are requiring computer ownership. Even if your child's school does not, we recommend purchasing a computer if you can manage it. It will make academic life easier. Time is as valuable to college students as to their parents (although students don't always budget their time effectively). It's much easier to crank out a long assignment in a dorm room than it is to fight over computers in one of the crowded clusters.

What kind to get? Check with your school's Office of Information Technology/Campus Computing. Different schools have different policies, and different students have different needs. Scientists and engineers will probably need more computing power than nurses and sales people because their applications require more memory, but all students should have access to the basics. We recommend getting as much computer as you can afford because it will more likely run tomorrow's new applications than a smaller, slower one with less memory. What about a printer? Again, it is much easier to print out something in a dorm room than to run across campus to one of the clusters. If you can afford it, get the printer too. In general, get guidance from the school in question.

DIVERSITY/GLOBAL MARKETPLACE. The workplace will become less exclusively populated by white males. Women, African-Americans, Hispanics, and Asian-Americans will assume more positions of leadership. There will be more immigrants in the American workplace. Business, moreover, will be conducted from a global perspective. Most of us did not work outside of the United States. Many of our children will.

Second and third languages will be an asset for them. More important than knowing other languages, however, will be a comfort born of attitude and experience with people different than themselves. The Rand Institute reported in 1994 that most colleges do NOT do a good job of preparing their graduates for the global economy. Language departments frequently focus on classical literature and devote no attention to newspapers and business letters. Conversational skills often suffer so that students can read Proust or Cervantes. Happily, there are a number of strategies which can help your sons or daughters meet the challenges this trend poses.

Study abroad is not a luxury or a frill. While not a requirement, it is a very useful building block in constructing a marketable career. The thing about study abroad is that students get the most out of it if they know the language of the nation they visit. If they hope to take classes in the language of the host country, they obviously must be relatively fluent in the language. This, in turn, means that college students should start preparing for study abroad their freshman year by mastering another language. (Happily, some of you are ahead of the curve in that you sent your high schoolers abroad in foreign exchange programs.) If a language house is available as a residence hall option, by all means encourage your son or daughter to take advantage of it. In a language house, students agree to speak only a particular foreign language while in the building. Since they're living there, fluency with the second or third language develops much more rapidly.

A variant of study abroad is work abroad. Internships and co-op jobs can provide splendid experience. AIESEC is an international work exchange organization that is active on 800 campuses in

86 countries with 80,000 members. In addition to arranging internships abroad, there is also training in business and leadership. (AIESEC is a French acronym for Association Internationale des Edutiants en Sciences Economiques et Commerciales. This roughly translates to Association of Economics and Commerce Students.)

Miller Templeton, who managed International Student Services and Programs at Georgia Tech for many years, is convinced that nothing takes the place of visiting other countries. Learning to deal with other currencies, transportation systems, telephone systems, passports, and security personnel are together an extremely important set of skills for tomorrow's citizen of the world. Tack on some language skills and an understanding of other cultures, and you have a level of cosmopolitan sophistication which will be highly marketable in today's global economy.

Fortunately, there are other, less challenging (and less expensive), methods that everyone can take advantage of. Most American colleges and universities have international students and faculty. If your sons and daughters will take the initiative, they can get to know individuals with differing cultural perspectives. Joining an international student organization can open up new vistas and make new connections. And anyone can take classes in other languages and about other cultures. Many colleges, in fact, require some minimum hours of study in this area.

KNOWLEDGE ECONOMY. Generally speaking, information and intelligence have always been an advantage in the competition to succeed. For the foreseeable future they will be requirements. We send our children to college for a variety of reasons, but surely one of the most important ones is so they will be able to make their way in the Information Age. If your child decides they're tired of Shakespeare and calculus, you might wish to draw it to their attention.

A degree does not an educated person make. What you really hope for is that your sons and daughters will become intellectually curious, learn how to learn, and, most importantly, love to learn throughout their lives. Colleges are not always successful in producing graduates with these qualities. If you possess these traits, chances are that your children will have been influenced by living with lovers of learning. At this stage in your relationship, there probably isn't much you can do to guarantee a "knowledgeable graduate."

CHANGE. Change is a virtual mantra in the business world. Most of us are loathe to embrace it, but we know it's in the air. If you asked incoming college students how many of them have had someone in their extended families who has been downsized out of a job, you would see lots of hands go up. Technological advances and global competition spur innovation. In other words, change is a constant. Our sons and daughters must learn to cope with it. Growing a resilient, self-sufficient college student is a complicated affair. Perhaps the best you can do is remind your children that life and work do change. The more relish with which you personally attack change, the more likely you are to promote psychological hardiness in your offspring.

COMPETITION. In a global economy, the United States competes with every other industrialized nation for customers. Developing nations are struggling to join the fray as serious contenders. Our country no longer produces VCR's. We lost that competition and the jobs that went with it. We continue to compete in the automotive industry with Japan and Europe. We continue to lead in the aerospace industry, but Japan, Europe, and China have other ideas about that. What does competition mean for our children? It means they will compete with engineers, scientists, and business people all over the world. It is a challenging world that our children face. When your son or daughter graduates and looks for a "real" job in the "real" world, employers will ask them about three broad categories: academics, activities, and work.

Academically, employers will look at grades and majors. In the long run, there is virtually no relationship between grades and professional success. We will tell you, however, that good grades from good schools do give a distinct advantage in the short run. Grades to employers suggest expertise, competence, and hard work. Employers frequently screen out graduating seniors with poor grades. Many employers have a GPA cut-off—3.0, 3.2, 3.5, or even higher. Where grades make the biggest difference is in opportunities for graduate or professional study. Your sons and daughters can't get into graduate school, medical school, law school, or business school without good grades. They can't get into the top schools without great grades. In a knowledge economy, knowledge is power. Advanced degrees increasingly are seen as testifying to expertise. In the knowledge economy, expertise bestows power. What all this adds up to is that good grades are an advantage. Many college students did not have to work hard to make good grades in high school. One of the most common miscalculations college students make is that they will make very good grades without working very hard to get them. They need to learn how to study a lot harder and smarter than they did before entering college. Learning Resource Centers and University 101 classes can help students make the transition from high school to college.

When employers ask about extracurricular activities, they're looking for people skills and intangibles related to character. Can the candidate get along with colleagues and customers? Can (s)he stand in front of others and make a persuasive and informative speech? Can they motivate others? Can they lead? Are they honorable, dependable, responsible? Can they juggle the demands of the classroom with co-curricular activities. For most employers, a high GPA with nothing to accompany it, is suspect. The student will likely be regarded as one-dimensional and impractical. This, of course, depends on the career aspirations of the particular student. Brilliant scientists, engineers, programmers, and accountants require fewer people skills than teachers and salespeople. Virtually any career, however, will flourish more readily with the ability to communicate effectively.

Many schools promote the development of a "co-curricular" transcript. By co-curricular is meant those campus activities that occur outside the classroom. Obviously, students can drown in activities, and maintaining a balance is important. Your sons or daughters should definitely take advantage, however, of the many opportunities for personal development which abound on virtually every college campus.

Regarding work, employers want to know that the candidate is not completely green. Do they have experience, especially experience in the field they're hoping to enter? Graduating with career-related experience under their belt is more important in today's competitive job market than ever. Accordingly, co-op jobs, internships, and the right summer or part-time jobs can provide a distinct advantage. Chances are, a strategically chosen, non-paying internship will prove a better investment for future careers than a paid job life-guarding or working in a summer camp. For students with liberal arts and social science degrees, work experience is especially important. A history major who worked on the school paper and was a stringer for a local paper is definitely in the running for a job in the field of journalism. An English major who interned in a publishing house or worked summers in an ad agency is also going to be competitive for jobs in those fields.

In addition to experience and skill building, there is also the important matter of contacts. Information about job openings, networking, and strong recommendations all depend upon who your sons and daughters know and who knows them.

TEAMWORK. Increasingly, employees are asked to collaborate with other employees, regardless of departments, to create high quality products and services in a short amount of time. The ability to follow, lead, and cooperate with various types of people will be an expectation in tomorrow's workplace. It's up to your son or daughter to cultivate these skills through activities, class projects, volunteerism, and study groups.

R.I.P. SECURE, LIFE-TIME JOB. The parents of today's college students have had several jobs and one or two careers. Your children may have many jobs and several careers. Constant change and intense global competition do not produce tranquil careers. Increasingly, employees' job security is directly tied to their contribution to organizational productivity. People aren't employed to fill a job; they are employed to solve a particular problem or complete a specific project. There will be more temps, independent contractors, and consultants. There will be fewer people who work for the same company for thirty years, then leave with a gold watch and a solid pension.

How do today's college students best prepare for tomorrow's unpredictable career paths? We tell our students to manage their careers entrepreneurially— whether or not they plan to start their own businesses. This means to expect change, if not virtual chaos, and it's up to them to adjust to that change. They, and no one else, are in charge of their careers.

They should begin cultivating a network of contacts by:

✓ forging alliances with professors and administrators

✓ cultivating relationships with colleagues and superiors in the workplace

✓ developing connections with other career-oriented students

✓ starting a network of contacts which they will cultivate and maintain throughout their lives

They should join a student professional society and become active in it. They should read key trade journals in their fields and stay abreast of changing trends. They should master all aspects of the job search—oral and written resume, interviewing, and how to find good job openings. I have heard one professor say that all students would be well served to attend a workshop on sales. Students are going to have to sell themselves effectively throughout their careers. They should work hard to stretch themselves outside of the classroom to develop communication and interpersonal skills. Effective leadership skills are money in the bank, but they are developed through hard work, trial and error, taking risks, and learning from experience. Probably most important, they should plan on learning new skills and technologies throughout their lives. They will need to if they want their careers to flouish.

FINDING DIRECTION. The challenge to find a career that fits provokes anxiety in student and parent alike. College students very much want to find meaningful careers. They also want financial security, and they have a vague sense of the volatile changes in the economy that make security such a rare commodity today. Parents are worried about squeezing four years of college into five or six. How will they pay for the extra tuition? And will their sons and daughters be able to support themselves after graduation? Indeed, we often find parents obsessed with their children's choice of major. Accounting, engineering, and nursing are seen as good because they translate directly into jobs. Humanities and social sciences are bad because they don't.

It is by no means a bad idea to consider the career potential of a major. On the other hand, students are NOT well served by majoring in accounting or computer science if they have no interest or ability in these areas. Conversely, English, art, and sociology can lead to productive careers in journalism, advertising, and criminal justice IF the student has a plan, gets some experience, and makes some contacts.

You may recall from Chapter 9, that young adults are forging an identity. A key component of that identity is their vocation—literally, their calling. Expect some false starts, some detours, and some setbacks. It is the exception, rather than the rule, for 18-year-olds to have their life's course figured out. The problem is not that your child goes through some perfectly normal vocational confusion, but that they become mired in it because of their passivity. We said at the beginning of this chapter that there is lots of professional career help for college students. There are also many steps which students can take on their own to help turn confusion, floundering, and anxiety into focus, progress, and confidence. Here are some resources they can use, and some steps you can encourage them to take.

# Resources

THE CAREER DEVELOPMENT CENTER (AKA THE PLACEMENT CENTER). This may be a part of the counseling center or a completely separate agency. Testing and counseling will be available, as well as a career library containing information about majors, careers, and companies that hire. This agency may assist students in finding employment. They probably offer workshops in job search techniques, resume writing, and interviewing.

THE COUNSELING CENTER (AKA THE MENTAL HEALTH CENTER, THE STUDENT DEVELOPMENT CENTER, THE CENTER FOR PSYCHOLOGICAL SERVICES). While some counseling centers treat only mental health problems, most provide career testing and counseling.

THE COOPERATIVE DIVISION. This department assists students in finding cooperative employment and internships.

THE MAIN LIBRARY. Librarians know many sources of information about vocational choosing and career planning. Some are books and periodicals, and some are on electronic databases or on the Internet.

THE INTERNET. Even a cursory search will turn up an infinitude of career-related material. Of course, Internet searches tend to overwhelm the user with a torrent of material, much of it useless. A good place to start is: <http://www.yahoo.com/Education/Guidance/Career_and_Employment_Planning/>. Encourage your student to click on The Career Key which provides an interactive introduction to career planning. Another useful site is <http://www.infoseek.com/Careers/Find_an_ideal_job/Explore_occupation?tid=10944&sv=N5> which has a number of helpful sites to choose from including the latest *Occupational Outlook Handbook* put out by the Department of Labor. Bear in mind that college students are going to be preoccupied with academics and social life when they first hit campus. The first week or even the first semester isn't the best time to offer unsolicited advice or assistance. You'll probably get a friendlier reception during the latter part of their first year, or even during their summer vacation.

ACADEMIC ADVISORS. The quality of the advice will obviously depend upon the particular advisor. Some can be extremely helpful in exploring career issues, particularly when the student is pursuing a career in the advisor's area. In some colleges, academic departments have departmental advisors who can provide information about the major and the career options to which it can lead.

THE FRESHMAN SEMINAR (AKA UNIVERSITY 101, FRESHMAN SURVIVAL, OR FRESHMAN SUCCESS COURSE). The emphasis is typically on study skills and adjusting to college, but many freshman seminars include a career component.

CAREER PLANNING SEMINAR. Many universities offer courses for credit on how to choose a major and select a career. Students will typically take career and personality tests, research majors and careers, and interview professors and practitioners out in the field.

THE ALUMNI ASSOCIATION. There will likely be a department that manages alumni relations. While it is not their primary mission to help undergraduates, this department can point your son or daughter to alumni in a particular field of interest. In some cases, mentoring programs are sponsored out of this office.

STEPS FOR STUDENTS TO TAKE. Not every student needs to take every step, but all students should take whatever steps necessary to accomplish three broad career related objectives:

1.  What are my interests, abilities, temperament, and values?

2.  What interests, abilities, temperament, and values are consistent with majors and careers I'm considering?

3.  What majors and careers best match my interests, abilities, temperament, and values?

Many of the following steps suggest themselves in the list of career planning resources above. We have listed them roughly in the order in which your student should take them.

1. Take the Freshman Seminar.

2. Scan the course offerings in the university catalog. First read the information about the colleges or schools that comprise the university. Georgia Tech, for example, is comprised of six

colleges: Engineering, Science, Architecture, Computing, DuPree College of Management, and the Ivan Alan College. When you find the college(s) that strike a responsive chord, read over the descriptions of those departments within it. Georgia Tech's College of Science contains departments of Chemistry, Physics, Mathematics, Biology, Earth & Atmospheric Science, Health & Performance Science, and Psychology. When you find the departments that spark your interest, read the course descriptions of the required courses. Gradually, you should be able to narrow down your range of alternatives to a manageable number.

3. Talk to students and professors in majors which interest you.

4. Go to the book store and scan some of the textbooks in the courses you'd need to take in order to pursue a particular major.

5. Visit departmental headquarters. Collect and study any available brochures. Talk with the departmental advisor.

6. Take an introductory course in a major under consideration. Many departments offer survey courses designed to acquaint students with the scope of the field and the careers which follow from it.

7. Interview practitioners in fields of interest. Interview co-op students with placements in fields of interest.

8. Take the Career Planning course.

9. Enroll in the Cooperative Education Plan (alternate study and work during a portion of your schooling). Yes, it may take longer to get your degree, but you'll be making money, getting experience, making contacts, and learning about the world of work. Co-ops typically make better grades while they're in school and get better jobs after they graduate. One

alumnus put it this way to a class full of freshmen: Of the top ten things I did in school to prepare me for the future, the first five were that I went co-op!

10. If you don't co-op, get an internship.

11. If you don't intern, get some kind of career-related work before you graduate.

12. Use the Career Development Center.

13. Use the Counseling Center.

14. Visit some meetings of relevant professional societies. As your plans start to crystallize, join the society that best fits you.

---

The Four Year Plan which follows is neither infallible nor divinely inspired. It is, however, an organized summary of what employers, recruiters, placement officers, and recent college graduates have told us. We believe it's worth discussing with your son or daughter.

The following plan for career success is taken from *Learning for the 21st Century* by Osher and Ward, also published by Kendall/ Hunt.

# Four Year Plan for Career Success

The citizen of the 21st century will think globally and plan strategically. You can start preparing right now by mapping out your strategy for getting the most out of college. Here is our Master Plan for using college as a springboard to success in the Information Age. Use it as a rough guide for creating your own plan.

# Freshman Year

Your first mission is to immerse yourself in the academic enterprise. Get organized. Become a serious student. Acquire basic computer skills. Begin to identify majors and careers of interest. Learn to manage stress. Start networking.

☑ **Develop Organizational Skills**

- ☐ Establish weekly schedule.
- ☐ Identify semester deadlines.
- ☐ Use To-Do list; prioritize and monitor daily.
- ☐ Master use of a planner.
- ☐ Develop a file system for school work and personal information.
- ☐ Organize an effective work space.

☑ **Develop Learning Skills**

- ☐ Learn how to use the library.
- ☐ Review material regularly.
- ☐ Learn effective reading, writing and notetaking techniques.
- ☐ Get to know your professors.
- ☐ Learn where to access "Word."

☑ **Master Computer Skills**

- ☐ Locate computer clusters.
- ☐ Know e-mail.
- ☐ Master a word processing program.
- ☐ Explore the Internet.
- ☐ Learn mathematics software if needed.

☑ **Finding Direction**

- ☐ Do a thorough self-assessment.
- ☐ Determine compatibility of majors to your interests and abilities.
- ☐ Explore various career fields.

- ☐ Investigate coursework required for different majors.
- ☐ Get career counseling as needed.
- ☐ Get advisement.
- ☐ Explore co-op and internships.
- ☐ Create resume disk.

## ☑ Stress Management Skills

- ☐ Develop an exercise program.
- ☐ Maintain a healthy diet and good sleeping habits.
- ☐ Learn to relax and keep perspective.

## ☑ Going Global

- ☐ Learn a language.
- ☐ Investigate "language house" living arrangements.
- ☐ Read about international events.
- ☐ Attend events sponsored by International Students Association

## ☑ Getting Involved

- ☐ Join a campus organization.

## ☑ Start Networking

- ☐ Connect with professors.
- ☐ Connect with alumni.
- ☐ Connect with people in field of interest.

# Sophomore Year

You use your organizational, learning, computer, and stress management skills throughout your collegiate career. You declare a major and begin to consider electives. You join a professional organization and contribute to it. You develop job search skills and secure career related employment.

☑ **Declare Major**

- ☐ Plan a schedule for taking required course work.
- ☐ Get to know your advisor.
- ☐ Look for electives that are compatible with your interests and complement your major.

☑ **Join Professional Associations**

- ☐ Join student chapter affiliated with your major.
- ☐ Attend local meetings regularly.
- ☐ Be as active as your schedule allows.
- ☐ Develop contacts by attending national meetings, conferences and/or seminars when convenient.

☑ **Expand Network of Contacts**

- ☐ Maintain current network.
- ☐ Develop new contacts.
- ☐ Use a Rolodex™ or other filing system.

☑ **Enhance Computer Skills**

- ☐ Learn spread sheet software.
- ☐ Learn graphics/presentation software.

☑ **Going Global**

- ☐ Live in a language house.

## ☑ Secure Career-Related Employment

- ☐ Begin co-op or part-time career-related job.
- ☐ Seek work assignments that will help develop skills in areas you are lacking.
- ☐ Develop contacts for mentoring and future employment.
- ☐ Learn all you can about this field and your fit within it.

## ☑ Develop Leadership Skills

- ☐ Volunteer for projects.
- ☐ Develop public speaking skills.
- ☐ Develop ability to manage projects.
- ☐ Learn how to run a meeting.
- ☐ Take a Leadership class.

## ☑ Develop Job Search Skills

- ☐ Reevaluate your marketable skills.
- ☐ Learn to express your skills effectively.
- ☐ Write a strong resume that stresses your skills.
- ☐ Attend job search workshops when available.
- ☐ Learn basics of interviewing for information.

# Junior Year

You assume more active and responsible positions in your extra-curricular activities. You cultivate contacts on and off campus. You learn more about your fields of interest. You find out about graduate and professional schools.

☑ **Evaluate Chosen Field**

- ☐ Keep up with your field through contacts and trade journals.
- ☐ Talk to your professors and employers.
- ☐ Visit your library, counseling center and placement office.
- ☐ Check out job qualifications necessary in your field.
- ☐ Continue co-op/internship.

☑ **Research Graduate or Professional Schools of Your Choice**

- ☐ Determine the benefits of an advanced degree in your field.
- ☐ Identify strong graduate programs.
- ☐ Apply for graduate or professional school entrance exams.

☑ **Continue Leadership Development**

- ☐ Enhance skills in communications and management.
- ☐ Attend Leadership workshops and seminars.
- ☐ Run for office or assume responsibility for a project.
- ☐ Develop contacts for mentoring and possible job leads.

☑ **Going Global**

- ☐ Select a Study Abroad program.

☑ **Keep Up With Computing**

- ☐ Learn key software applications.

# Senior Year

You're almost there! Apply for graduate programs and take entrance exams if you plan to get an advanced degree. Gear up for the job search by revising your resume and preparing for interviews.

## ☑ Take Graduate or Professional School Entrance Exams

- ☐ Prepare for exams thoroughly.
- ☐ Check campus resources for available preparatory programs.
- ☐ Check bookstores and library for preparatory books.
- ☐ Arrive at test site early and well rested. Be prepared for 3–4 hour test session.

## ☑ Arrange for Interviews through Campus Placement Office

- ☐ Attend programs explaining procedures of placement office.
- ☐ Follow all procedures carefully.
- ☐ Maintain contact with Placement Office staff.

## ☑ Write a Winning Resume

- ☐ Develop a clear job objective.
- ☐ Detail skills or experience using the STAR Technique.
- ☐ Tailor your resume to the company or graduate school you are interviewing.
- ☐ Highlight key words and phrases that are your biggest selling points.

## ☑ Get References

- ☐ Decide who can give you the strongest references.
- ☐ Talk to references about possible job leads.
- ☐ Inform your references about your strongest selling points.
- ☐ Supply references with copy of your resume.

☑ **Apply to Graduate Schools.**

or

☑ **Look for Permanent Employment**

- ☐ Tap network of contacts.
- ☐ Look for opportunities to develop new skills in learning organizations.
- ☐ Develop strategy for expressing match of company's or graduate school's needs to your interests and abilities.

☑ **Master the Interviewing Process**

- ☐ Research typical questions you might be asked.
- ☐ Prepare effective questions to ask the interviewer.
- ☐ Role play upcoming interviews with friends. Ask for feedback.
- ☐ Send thank-you notes to each interviewer.

☑ **Take Plant Trips or Visit Grad Schools**

- ☐ Investigate what happens during the plant trip or in the graduate school selection process.
- ☐ Send any requested additional information.

☑ **Evaluate Offers**

- ☐ Determine what your needs are versus what the company or graduate school has to offer.
- ☐ Seek guidance, if necessary.
- ☐ Choose the best offer.

# Students
# Who Commute

There are distinct advantages to students living on campus, but it's not for everyone. Some colleges and universities have no residence halls. Some families can't afford room and board. Some students have special needs because of disabilities that are best met at home. A few simply may not be mature enough as yet to leave home. Whatever the reasons, there are unique challenges to parenting a college student who lives at home.

Much of the challenge has to do with your son's or daughter's growing independence. College students are considered adults, at least they are if they're over seventeen years of age. They can vote and join the armed services. If they violate a law, they can be prosecuted as adults. And there's the Buckley Amendment which we discussed in Chapter 9. Without a student's permission, colleges are forbidden by law to divulge information about that student to anyone—including family.

College can be doubly trying for families with commuting students. Your sons or daughters are on their own all day. They're meeting new friends, exposed to new cultures, and facing new, sometimes unsettling, ideas. They must make their own decisions. Then, after being an adult all day, they must return to their homes. When we say they're adults during the day, we realize that not all freshmen (or seniors for that matter) are emotionally and mentally mature. We do mean to say that it can be confusing to young men and women to analyze Shakespeare and learn differential equations in the afternoon and come home to be pestered about cleaning up their room. Here are some of the key issues you'll probably face.

## Key Issues

CURFEWS. This was probably an issue in high school. It's likely to be a bigger issue in college. Families vary drastically on this topic. Some parents provide a key and ask not to be disturbed regardless of the hour, but many find it very difficult to sleep until they know their sons and daughters have safely returned home. You can expect your student to compare notes with other students on this and myriad other topics on campus. Our own belief is to accord the commuting student plenty of freedom, but to expect a matching amount of responsibility. You'd like a general idea of when they'll return and want to be called past a certain hour. As your student progresses through college and advances in age, you are well served to accord more freedom to him or her.

CHORES. Your student will be in class for fewer hours than when in high school, but should be spending more time studying. It is reasonable to expect students to contribute to the running of the household—meals, dishes, housecleaning, etc. Be considerate, however, of their academic obligations. Just because they're not in class, doesn't mean they're not busy. Be wary of jeopardizing their scholastic standing by weighing them down with childcare and household chores "since they now have so much free time." It is not possible to study effectively and simultaneously care for a hyperactive preschooler. The key to this issue and most others is to communicate straightforwardly about what you expect, hear their side of the story, and reach a compromise you both can live with.

FAMILY INVOLVEMENT. It is normal for your son or daughter increasingly to pursue a life of their own. It is normal for you to want to retain close contact with your son or daughter. Expect that they will want to enjoy a social life revolving around eighteen and nineteen-year-olds. Expect less family life which includes them. Do encourage them to bring friends and dates over for meals, snacks, television, and "hanging out"—if you're comfortable with casual entertaining. Do propose periodic occasions which include their favorite meal or restaurant. Do ask them about their school and their life. Don't probe or interrogate. Do listen to what they have to tell you.

STUDY TIME/STUDY SPACE. In order for college students to perform effectively they need some peace and quiet. Try to agree on a regular period of time when they have no responsibilities or obligations. Indeed, this can be an indirect way of encouraging conscientious studying. If the family is large and there is lots of commotion in your home, support their decision to spend time in the college library or study lounges. Their top priority is to learn as much as they can.

EXTRACURRICULAR ACTIVITIES. One of the reasons college administrators like students to live on campus is because such students are more likely to get involved in campus activities—professional societies, charitable work, and various social, artistic, and recreational clubs. We know that extracurricular involvement promotes leadership development, citizenship, and the ability to work collaboratively. If this sounds too flowery to you, we can assure you that most employers take this stuff very seriously. They will ask your son or daughter about their campus activities and what they learned from them.

Some universities promote "co-curricular transcripts" to certify a student's involvement in a range of activities which promote a variety of highly marketable skills. You might find it reassuring that your son or daughter spends the minimal amount of time on campus and is generally around the house or with old high school friends. This is a common pattern for many commuters, but it does not promote academic or professional success. Encourage your child to use the library, join study groups, and participate in some campus activities. They will be a lot better off if they do.

WORK. A college education costs a lot of money. (But if you think education is expensive, ignorance costs even more!) For that reason, your son or daughter may need to work in order to finance school. There are some distinct advantages to working your way through school, or contributing substantially to it. Your son or daughter will appreciate it all the more. They will less likely treat it cavalierly. Not many students like to spend thousands of their own hard earned dollars to flunk out. The workplace itself can provide a challenging environment which promotes personal and professional development. Students can learn self-discipline and responsibility. They can learn about the business world. They can learn people skills. They can make contacts. And more than one student has learned that they will study as hard as it takes to get the degree that will be their ticket out of a dead-end job because that's often the only kind of job available to them.

On the other hand, it does not make sense to us for someone to work 40 hours a week on top of a full academic load of demanding classes at a competitive university. Chances are good their grades will be low, and that rules out graduate or professional school. Often times a student is better served to take an extra year or so. It usually helps them keep their grades and spirits up. We know of no law that requires someone to start their career at twenty-one instead of twenty-three. College loans are certainly not frivolous matters, but they often are a reasonable part of an overall strategy for success.

We also remind you that the most useful work for any student is career-related. Urge your son or daughter to investigate co-op jobs and internships if they must work to make ends meet.

# Campus Jargon
## im•por•tant vo•cab•u•lary

Colleges and their students use English with a generous smattering of "Collegese." Some of the terms are unique to a particular campus, but the words in this list should be fairly common to most schools.

**All Nighter**—Staying up all night to study for an exam or to write a paper.

**Blow-Off Course**—A course that has the reputation for being especially easy.

**Blue Book**—A thin booklet with blank pages and a blue cover that is used when students write essay examinations. They are available at most college bookstores.

**CA/RA**—A Community Advisor or Resident Advisor is an undergraduate student on each residence hall floor responsible for the residents on that floor.

**Care Package**—An unexpected package filled with goodies from home.

**Catalog**—A book that contains course numbers and descriptions as well as other academic information.

**Computer Lab**—A room filled with computers for all students to use.

**Co-op**—The Cooperative Program allows students to alternate semesters/quarters working and going to school.

**Cume**—The cumulative grade point average.

**Dead Week**—The week prior to exam week when most campus extracurricular activities stop and students begin studying for exams.

**Double Major**—Students with two majors.

**Drop/Add**—The time period that may last from one day to one week where students can drop or add courses to their schedules for the upcoming semester.

**E-mail**—Electronic mail; a popular way for students, faculty, staff and parents to communicate.

**Fees**—Costs other than tuition or room and board (student activity fee, computer fee, health fee).

**Formal**—A dressy affair, usually a fraternity or sorority party.

**ID**—The student identification card used for meals, purchases at the bookstore or general identification.

**IFC**—The Interfraternity Council is the governing board for fraternities.

**Meal Plan**—A meal plan is a set number of meals a student buys per week. The number of meals may range from 10 to 14 to 21 and is paid at the beginning of each semester.

**Minor**—A minor is a specialization in an area that requires fewer hours than a major.

**Panhel**—The Panhellenic Council is the governing board for sororities.

**Pass/Fail**—Students are allowed to take a limited number of courses (not in their major) pass/fail. They either pass or fail, but they don't receive a letter grade.

**Pre-req**—A class that a student must take BEFORE (s)he is qualified to take a higher-level class.

**R**—This letter denotes Thursday in the schedule of courses booklets.

**Res Life**—The Office of Residence Life.

**RHA**—The Residence Hall Association is the student governing board for residence halls.

**RHC**—Residence Hall Coordinators are graduate students or full time staff who live in each residence hall.

**Rush**—To apply for membership in a fraternity or sorority.

**SGA**—The Student Government Association.

**Syllabus**—A list of class requirements, grading procedures, assignments and other information given to students by professors the first day of class.

**TA**—A Teaching Assistant assists a professor in teaching. TAs are usually upperclassmen or graduate students.

**Take Home**—An exam given by a professor to be completed outside of class.

**Transcript**—An official document produced by the college/ university that records grades and grade point averages.

# More to Read

## Financial Aid

Davis, Herm & Kennedy, Joyce. *College Financial Aid for Dummies*, IDG Books, 1997.

A readable and user-friendly guide through the maze of opportunities and obstacles.

Osborn, Michael T. (Editor). *The Best Resources for College Financial Aid*, 1996/97.

Describes each resource (books, websites, CD-ROMs, etc.) and recommends the most useful for the various steps in finding scholarships and financial aid.

Van Dusen, William et al. *10 Minute Guide to Paying for College*, Arco, 1996.

A quick and easy guide to the basics.

## Study Skills

Armstrong, William & Lampe, M. Willard. *Study Tactics*, Barron's Educational Series, 1983.

This book teaches students to improve study techniques, take tests with confidence and master time management.

Jensen, Eric. *Student Success Secrets*, Barron's Educational Series, 1996.

Students will learn study skills tips, how to retain information, how to take good notes and how to score high on exams.

Pauk, Walter. *How to Study in College*, Houghton Mifflin Co., 1996.

A tad dry, but clear, thorough, and sound.

Silver, Theodore. *Study Smart*, Villard Books, 1995.

Hand-on, nuts-and-bolts techniques for earning higher grades.

## Freshman Success

Ellis, Dave. *The Master Student*, McGraw-Hill, 1997.

Readable and encouraging to students, the book covers the how-to's of a variety of topics related to collegiate success.

Gardner, John. *Your College Experience*. Wadsworth, 1997.

Experts from various fields (learning centers, the library, the career center) explain their domains. Reads like a textbook—comprehensive and understandable, but a little dry.

Osher, Bill & Ward, Joann. *Learning for the 21st Century*, 5th edition, Dubuque, Iowa: Kendall/Hunt, 1998.

Written in a conversational style, the authors connect each topic they cover to students' number one concern—career success.

# Young Adult Development

Coburn, Karen Levin & Treeger, Madge Lawrence. *Letting Go*. Adler & Adler, 1992.

Written by college counselors, the book explores the developing personality of the college student and the changing psychological relationship between students and their parents.

Chickering, Arthur & Reisser, Linda. *Education and Identity*. Josey-Bass, 1993.

Virtually every dean of students read an earlier edition of this in graduate school. It may tell you more than you need to know about young adult development, and you probably don't want to buy this tome. You might want to check it out of a library, however, and read over what your son or daughter is going through.

# Georgia Institute of Technology

# Resource Guide

The following pages are designed to provide you with specific information about the programs and activities at Georgia Tech. This guide is not designed to give complete information about each topic, rather to give you the highlights and important facts about each area. We have tried to make all dates, fees and regulations as current as possible. However, this information is in a constant process of revision. If you have any doubts or questions about this information, feel free to contact the specific department or program for more information.

Most of the information for this resource guide was taken from the Guide to Student Life and the Georgia Tech Catalog.

# TIMELINE OF EVENTS ••••••••••••••••

The following is a timeline of important dates and deadlines.

## March

1—Financial Aid deadline

## May

1—GT Acceptance Deposit of $250 due

1—Residence Hall Application and Deposit of $120 due

20—Receive FASET Orientation Materials

## June

 Mail Medical Records to the Student Health Center

Have your student's high school send final transcripts to Tech

Have any AP scores or joint enrollment grades sent to Tech

## July

Sign-up for a meal plan

Be on the look-out for great computer bargains

Sign up for sorority rush

AP Scores due

## August

22—Tuition and fees due for Fall Quarter

# THIS IS GEORGIA TECH: CAMPUS DEMOGRAPHICS ••••••••••

## General Information

- undergraduates—9,594
- graduates—3,492
- faculty—672 full-time
- in-state—53.7%
- out-state—46.3%

## Gender

- men—9,547
- women—3,539

## Ethnicity

- Asian—2,056
- African-American—1,156
- Hispanic—456
- Native American—26
- Multi-racial—89

## College

- Ivan Allen College—600
- College of Sciences—1,321
- College of Engineering—8,017
- College of Computing—1,144
- College of Architecture—779
- Dupree College of Management—1,108

# FINANCIAL AID ••••••••••••••••••••••••

The Office of Student Financial Planning and Services administers all scholarships, loans, federal grants, and work-study programs for undergraduate students and produces a brochure describing the various types of financial aid available.

New or transfer students wanting need-based aid should submit the Georgia Tech Application for Financial Aid and file the FAFSA with the federal processor no later than **March 1.** To follow up on applications or obtain additional information, students can check with a financial aid counselor.

Short-term, temporary assistance, and emergency loans are available for students at the beginning of each quarter. Guidelines for this type of assistance are available through the Office of Student Financial Planning and Services.

## Scholarships Available at Georgia Tech

✓ The Hope Scholarship

✓ The Presidents Scholarship

✓ Governors Scholarship

✓ The Scholarships and Financial Aid Office can give you a complete book of scholarships available for Georgia Tech students.

# Grants Available at Georgia Tech

✓ Georgia Tech Grant

✓ Federal Pell Grant

✓ Supplemental Educational Opportunity Grant (SEOG)

✓ Student Incentive Grant (SIG)

# Loans Available at Georgia Tech

✓ Stafford Student Loan

✓ Parent Loan for Undergraduate Students (PLUS)

✓ Perkins Loan

✓ Short-term and Emergency Loans

# Financial Deadlines to Remember

✓ The Georgia Tech Application for Financial Aid is due March 1.

✓ The Free Application for Federal Student Aid (FAFSA) is due March 1.

✓ The Admissions deposit is $250 and is due May 1.

✓ The Housing deposit is $120 and is due May 1.

✓ Tuition and fees for Fall Semester 1999 are due the latter part of August. (Exact date was not set when this book went to press.)

For more information on scholarships, loans or financial aid, contact the Office of Student Financial Planning and Scholarships.

# Tuition and Fees
# for 1999–2000 .....................

|  | Resident of Georgia | Nonresident of Georgia |
|---|---|---|
| Semester Fees |  |  |
| Matriculation | $ 1,213 | $ 1,213 |
| Nonresidence | $ 0 | $ 3,639 |
| Transportation | $ 40 | $ 40 |
| Student Activity | $ 75 | $ 75 |
| Health Service | $ 107 | $ 107 |
| Athletic | $ 50 | $ 50 |
| Technology | $ 75 | $ 75 |
| Subtotal | $ 1,560 | $ 5,199 |
| Books and Supplies | $ 450 | $ 450 |
| Room and Board | $ 2,850 | $ 2,850 |
| Personal Expenses (clothing, laundry, recreation, travel, etc) | $ 750 | $ 750 |
| Total per Semester | $ 5,610 | $ 9,249 |
| Total per Year | $ 11,220 | $ 18,497 |

TRANSPORTATION FEE COVERS: use of the Stinger and Stingerette shuttle services.

STUDENT ACTIVITY FEE COVERS: student government initiatives; recreation center: building, upkeep, equipment; student programs: films, cultural events, concerts.

ATHLETIC FEE COVERS: tickets to athletic events.

HEALTH SERVICES FEE COVERS: flu shots, x-rays, office visits, equipment rental, some prescriptions.

TECHNOLOGY FEE COVERS: computers on campus, printers, software, TAs, paper, ink cartridges, maintenance, use of e-mail.

## Average Price per Semester

| Residence Hall | $1,343–$1,951 |
|---|---|
| Greek House | $550 |
| Apartment | $800 |

# RESIDENCE LIFE •••••••••••••••••••••••

Georgia Tech is a residential campus community with approximately half of all full-time students in attendance living in residential facilities. Such facilities have commonly been known as "dormitories"—places where students eat and sleep. Residential living has a great impact on the quality of both undergraduate and graduate life on campus and has a direct influence on the total education of students.

One of the most important growth opportunities provided by the institute is the chance to live in a residential community. The environment is unique—totally different from any you have experienced in the past or will experience in the future. During the college years students usually undergo a period of intense intellectual, emotional and physical growth. A student grows and develops not only in the academic classroom but 24 hours a day. What a student learns in his or her out-of-class life is of great importance to the attitudes, aspirations, motivations, and level of achievement demonstrated in the classroom. The residential environment enhances and supplements the classroom experience.

Students living on campus are exposed to life styles, beliefs, attitudes and values often much different from their own. Through interaction among peers, significant issues are questioned, confronted and investigated. Students are frequently challenged to clarify, change and build their own personal system of values and beliefs. The result of this testing and clarifying is hopefully the development of a personally valid set of values.

## Freshmen Experience Program

Freshmen at Georgia Tech are not required to live on campus unless they are part of the Freshmen Experience Program. The majority of freshmen participate in the Freshmen Experience (FE) Program designed to help incoming freshmen get as much out of their educational experience at Tech as possible. Data collected from recent FE years suggests that FE participants have higher grade point averages, adjust to college life more quickly, and develop stronger support networks and friends than freshmen who do not participate in FE.

# Housing Specifics:

## SIZE

The size of most residence hall rooms at Tech range from 12' x 10' to 16' x 12'.

## ROOMMATES

The Department of Housing will send your student the name(s) of his/her roommate(s) by early September.

## VOICE MAIL

Georgia Tech does not provide voice mail in the residence hall rooms. If your student wants an answering machine, s(he) should bring one from home.

## LOFTS

Some residence halls have lofts that are already built into the rooms. Check with the Department of Housing for specifics on lofts.

## CARPET

Residence halls at Georgia Tech are not carpeted. Check with your students roommate to decide on carpet.

## MICROWAVE

Microwaves are allowed in residence hall rooms at Tech. Most floors have microwaves in their kitchenettes for students to use.

## CARS

Freshmen who live on campus are not allowed to register a vehicle during their first quarter at Georgia Tech.

# ORIENTATION ••••••••••••••••••••••••••

FASET Orientation is the orientation program for new students and their parents/guardians. FASET stands for the "Familiarization and Adaptation to the Surroundings and Environs of Tech." At FASET Orientation, new students become a part of Tech by interacting with other students, faculty and staff in small and large groups. Students will plan an academic program with an advisor, complete all registration procedures, and discover and experience the Tech environment.

At Tech, we realize that families are in transition when students leave home for college. An orientation to Tech life is important to help parents/guardians understand and support their son or daughter through the various changes and experiences that students encounter at Tech. Although traditional freshmen need to make their own decisions, we know they can use parental support. Therefore, many of the FASET Orientation activities are offered to both students and parents. Several sessions are for parents only, some are for students only. To alleviate concerns and questions, there will be opportunities for parents to talk to current Tech students, faculty, and staff. Parents/guardians will also learn about the many services and opportunities available and how they can assist their student to make a successful transition to college life.

There are four different sessions between July 18 and August 19, 1999 from which you may choose one to attend. Each two-day session is designed to help you become a part of the Tech community. Your student will receive information in early June about the exact FASET Orientation dates and the program. At that time, your student can preference a FASET Orientation session to attend.

The Fall Quarter FASET Orientation Dates for 1999 are:

July 18–19

July 25–26

August 1–2

August 18–19

In addition, your student may participate in the activities of R.A.T.S. Week (Recently Acquired Tech Students). R.A.T.S. Week is August 23–27, 1999 and is designed to provide optional activities and programs for students to attend before classes begin. R.A.T.S. Week activities include: Freshmen Convocation, Caribbean Dinner, Traditions Night, pool party at SAC, outdoor movies, cosmic bowling, MARTA Tag, shuttles to grocery stores and many more activities!

# Student Life •••••••••••••••••••••••

## Assistance for Persons with Disabilities

Through the Access Disabled Assistance Program for Tech Students (A.D.A.P.T.S.), Georgia Tech offers self-identified student with disabilities assistance with registration, academic advisement, accessibility, transportation, parking, housing, counseling, tutoring, taped textbooks, advocacy, test proctoring, referral services and other needs. The office sponsors a student advisory club and promotes disability awareness programs for departmental faculty and staff, and student organizations. Interpreting services for deaf and hard-of-hearing students are available through the interpreter coordinator.

## Bicycles

Bicycle registration is not required, but is advised, and can be done at the Campus Police headquarters free of charge. It is also a good idea to invest in a bike lock.

## Bookstore and Mall

The Georgia Tech Bookstore, located adjacent to the Student Center, provides students with textbooks, school supplies and equipment for each quarters work. The bookstore orders equipment, such as drawing instruments and calculators, to meet faculty-approved standards and recommends that students wait until reaching campus to make such purchases.

Also available from the bookstore:

> personal and toilet articles
>
> Georgia Tech souvenirs
>
> shirts and Georgia Tech active wear

stationery and gifts

residence hall supplies

reference works and study guides

a large selection of paperbacks and general books

Next to the Bookstore the Georgia Tech Mall houses a diverse group of retail operations, including:

Burdell's General Store (a convenience store)

Hair Cuttery

American Express Travel Agency

Campus One-Card Office

cyber.cafe@gatech (coffee house)

College Optical

The Georgia Tech Bookstore provides a check cashing service for all students currently enrolled. Students may cash checks for any amount up to $50 per day by presenting their Buzz Card and current fees receipt. There is a 25¢ fee for this service.

ATMs are on the first and second floors of the Student Center for the regional banks Wachovia, NationsBank, and Lockheed Georgia Credit Union, and national networks of Avail, Honor, Cirrus, Plus, Visa, MasterCard and Discover.

## Career Services

Career Services offers students a variety of services, from helping to choose a career to finding part-time and full-time employ-ment. The office provides career counseling and testing; career planning and development information; seminars on resume writing, interviewing, business etiquette, networking, job search strategies, how to use the career library, etc.; videotaped "mock interviews;" cover letter and resume critiques; internship, part-time and full-time job listings; literature and videos on over 700 companies and government agencies; salary surveys; lists of recruiting companies and organizations; company contact information; graduate school information; and resume referral services.

Campus recruiting takes place each quarter. Approximately 600 employers, representing a substantial number of the Fortune 500 corporations, recruit on campus annually. A resume book, consisting of graduating seniors' resumes, is available to interested employers.

## Counseling Center

The Counseling Center's professional counselors and psychologists assist in a confidential manner with academic, career, and personal concerns whenever students request counseling services. The Center's career counseling helps students examine and work towards resolving personal and interpersonal issues related to selecting a major or career. The Center's library provides information through reference books, videos, a computer-assisted career decision-making program, catalogs from other colleges and business and graduate schools, and a number of tests for determining occupational interests, abilities, and personality traits.

## Dining Service

Tech's computerized meal programs work much like a checking account. At many times during the quarter, students may deposit money to set up their meal plan account. Whenever students eat at any of the campus dining locations, they simply present their meal card, and the amount of the purchase will automatically be deducted from their account.

Meal programs eliminate the need to have cash on hand for meals. At the end of the quarter, any declining balance remaining in the meal plan account can be carried over into the following quarters throughout the year. Students may use meal programs at any of these campus dining locations:

## THE STUDENT CENTER FOOD COURT

Located in the middle level of the Student Center, the food court serves meals throughout the calendar year. This facility features Burger King®, Chick-fil-A® and Freshens®, as well as daily specials selected from the salad bar, deli line, Mexican foods, fresh desserts, beverage line and hot food line.

## WOODRUFF'S

Located in Woodruff Hall, the dining hall provides board plan meals for the Freshman Experience as well as upperclassmen on the west side of campus. The meal plan provides a wide array of foods for breakfast, lunch, dinner, and late evening dinner.

## JUNIOR'S GRILL

Located on the Hill, Junior's features a grill dining experience and cafeteria-style service.

## BRITTAIN DINING HALL

Brittain Dining Hall provides board plan meals for the Freshman Experience. The meal plan provides a wide variety of foods for breakfast, brunch, lunch, dinner and late evening meals.

## FERST PLACE RESTAURANT

Ferst Place features a hot and cold luncheon buffet and is located on the third floor of the Student Center.

## McDonald's

McDonald's® is located in the Coliseum and the Athletic Association Building.

## West Side Diner

This is located across from Woodruff hall in the parking deck. The Diner is open every day from 8:00 p.m.–2:00 a.m.

## The Catering Office

This office is located on the third floor of the Student Center and provides catering services for all members of the Tech community.

## The Athletic Association Dining Hall

Located on the second floor of the Edge Building, this dining hall serves only breakfast and lunch to the general student population. All meals are prepared with nutritional content in mind for the athletic body.

# Diversity Issues and Programs

The Office of Diversity Issues and Programs is responsible for fostering a vision of diversity appreciation, reflective of the

 Institute's strategic plan, which enables students from all backgrounds and cultures to thrive and succeed at Tech. The office provides an institutionalized approach for meeting the co-curricular needs of underrepresented populations by coordinating and planning educational opportunities that enhance interaction and learning across groups. Through intentional educational programming, the office assists the campus in tolerating, embracing and appreciating Tech's rich cultural diversity.

## Fraternities and Sororities

The 40 social fraternities and sororities are coordinated by Student Affairs. These groups offer a variety of activities, opportunities and services to the Georgia Tech community.

## Identification Cards (Buzz Card)

All students receive a Georgia Tech photo identification card, called a Buzz Card. Buzz Cards entitle students to special privileges as members of the Georgia Tech community, including discounts at the Georgia Tech Mall computer store and discount tickets at Tick-A-Tech. Students must present their Buzz Cards upon request to Institute administrators, the Library, SAC, athletic events and special functions.

## International Student Services and Programs

The ISSP Department provides services for two groups: over 1,000 international students from approximately 90 countries; and international exchange visitors. These students and exchange visitors receive assistance in maintaining status with the U.S. immigration and naturalization service and in adjusting to Georgia Tech and American Society. In return, many students and exchange visitors work with the ISSP staff to develop programs promoting intracultural understanding.

## OMED: Educational Services

OMED is an academic services organization that seeks to assist Georgia Tech in its development of the complete learner who is a gifted African-American, Native American, Latino, or Hispanic. This complete development is intended to ensure that these students become inspired, high performing problem solvers. When they graduate or leave Tech their choice set is optimal and they, as well as their families, will have had a positive and gratifying experience.

## Post Office

The Post Office staff will assign a campus post office box to each student. This box will be the student's permanent mailing address while at Georgia Tech. All official Institute mail goes to the student's Georgia Tech box; students are  responsible for checking mail boxes each day. Students should be aware that they may share mailboxes with one other student.

Students planning to be away from campus for the summer or for extended periods of time should notify the post office of a forwarding address. Students (including co-ops) wishing to use their post office boxes while not enrolled must notify the post office of their intentions via cyber.

## The Stinger

Georgia Tech's on-campus bus service, the Stinger, operates Monday through Friday from 7:00 a.m. until 1:00 a.m. and Sundays from 6:00 p.m. until 1:00 a.m. when the Institute is in session. Each route takes approximately 15 minutes to complete, and there are stops in most academic and housing areas.

## The Stingerette Escort Service

The Stingerette Escort Service supplements the Stinger bus service. A van operated by Georgia Tech students provides transportation to students who cannot be served by the regular bus system. During the day the Stingerette Service provides transportation for mobility-impaired students, and during the evening hours, 6:00 p.m. to 4:00 a.m. the Stingerette provides an escort service to students not on the evening Stinger bus route.

Stinger schedules and route information are available at the Campus Police Department and Parking Office.

The Fuller E. Callaway III student athletic complex (SAC) houses all campus recreational facilities as well as the Campus Recreation Department. Facilities include: a 50-meter outdoor pool, bubble-covered pool, and the Olympic Aquatic Center with diving well; six multi-purpose courts for basketball, volleyball, and badminton; eight indoor racquetball and two squash  courts; a cardiotheater with aerobic conditioning equipment (Stairmaster, treadmills, Concept II rowing machines); and a weight room with free weights and machines. SAC is open daily with the exception of home football games and holidays.

## STUDENT CENTER

The Fred B. Wenn Student Center is located in the heart of the Georgia Tech Campus and services Tech Students many service needs. Governed and run by students, the Student Center Program Council consists of student-run planning committees that organize and coordinate campus-wide activities and events. The Student Center houses a post office; bowling, billiards and video games; a crafts center; the Community Service Office; a music listening room; a ballroom; several smaller meeting rooms; a credit union; a 200-seat theater; a Mac Lab; lounge and study areas; and three dining options. Vans, a cellular phone, and audio/visual equipment are available for use by student organizations through the Student Center Administration Office. Also located in the Student Center is the Center for the Arts Box Office, offering students discounted tickets to a variety of entertainment options.

The hours of operation for many of the Student Center Services vary, however the Student Center building is open 24 hours to provide students a place to meet and study at any hour.

## Student Government

The Georgia Tech undergraduate and Graduate Student Government Associations enable students to maintain responsible and respected self-government and official institutional involvement in academic and nonacademic affairs.

## Student Publications and Radio

The student publications and radio communications board oversees the budgeting and operation of the *Technique*, the official student newspaper; the *Blueprint*, the student yearbook; and other student publications, in addition to the operation of the student radio station, WREK 91.1 FM.

Other student publications include the *North Avenue Review*, an open forum magazine, and *Erato*, the student literary magazine.

## Study Abroad

The Study Abroad Office (SAO) serves as a centralized point for information regarding Georgia Tech, the University System, and other institution's study abroad programs. In order to prepare students for the "global marketplace" of the twenty-first century, Georgia Tech offers numerous, diverse programs to study for a quarter or longer in another country and receive Tech credit courses completed. Tech now has exchange programs in countries across the globe which allow students to pay Tech tuition, continue receiving financial aid, and transfer credit toward a Tech degree. SAO will advise students about everything from program options and financial aid procedures to credit transfers, visas, and international health insurance. Anyone who wishes to be in the vanguard rather than the rear guard of a world where more and more employers value international experience should consider studying abroad. For more information contact the Study Abroad Office.

The mission of the Women's Resource Center is to enhance the academic performance and personal development of the women at Georgia Tech by striving to create a more inclusive and supportive campus environment for women, and by promoting understanding among Georgia Tech's diverse community of women and men.

# FRATERNITIES AND SORORITIES ......

## Interfraternity Council

The Interfraternity Council (IFC) is the governing body for all 32 fraternities. The Interfraternity Council is comprised of five executive officers and several committees. Each fraternity has a representative on IFC. The fraternities at Georgia Tech offer unique opportunities. Brotherhood, scholarship, philanthropy, and social activities are at the heart of the Greek system.

## Panhellenic Council

Panhellenic Council is the governing body for all eight sororities at Tech and unites every sorority woman regardless of individual affiliation. The Council is headed by the eight executive board members and each sorority on campus has a delegate on the Panhellenic Council. Together, the Council members strive for overall Greek unity, while working together to unite sorority women and strengthen their values through cooperation, common interests, talents, and skills brought from each sisterhood.

Together the Interfraternity Council and Panhellenic Council are responsible for promoting scholarship, philanthropy, personal growth, safety, and campus involvement in Greek life and the Greek community as a whole. They work diligently to make the Greek community a positive and active influence on the Tech campus and in the community.

Information on fraternity and sorority rush will be mailed to students in the summer. For more information, call the Greek Life Office.

# STUDENT HEALTH CENTER • • • • • • • • • •

The mission of the Student Health Center is to provide the
Tech community with a premier health service program founded
on sound quality improvement principles, that will match the
demographic and diverse medical and health educational needs
of the students.

The Student Health Center is an ambulatory health care clinic
that provides medical care and health education for eligible
students and spouses. It is located in the Joseph B. Whitehead
Building across from the Russ Chandler Baseball Stadium.

The staff consists of general practice, family practice and internal
medicine physicians, nurse practitioners, registered nurses,
medical and radiological technologists, pharmacists and health
educators. Services at the Health Center are rendered in the
Primary Care Center and in the Wellness Center.

The Primary Care Center employs full-time staff physicians,
consulting physicians in gynecology, orthopedics, psychiatry,
radiology, ENT, dermatology, as well as nurse practitioners,
RN's, pharmacists, and medical and radiological technicians. The
staff is trained in family, internal and emergency medicine and
have experience in all areas of primary care medicine including
the previously mentioned areas and minor surgical problems.
A women's health nurse practitioner is available for gynecologi-
cal problems and preventive care, such as Pap smears. All clini-
cal staff are available for contraceptive counseling and sexually
transmitted disease prevention and treatment.

The Wellness Center is available to all Tech students, and offers
computer-assisted health and nutritional assessments, wellness
seminars and events, an information resources center, and personal consultations.

# Medical Entrance Form

Students received a Medical Entrance Form with their letter of acceptance. All students should complete the form and mail it to the Student Health Center before registration. In addition to the Medical Entrance Form, students must provide evidence of updated immunization certificate and tuberculosis screening. Completed forms must be mailed to:

Student Health Services
Georgia Institute of Technology
Atlanta, GA 30332-0470
Attention: Medical Record Department

## Immunization Screening

In accordance with recommendations from the Centers for Disease Control (CDC), all students entering Tech will be screened for tuberculosis. Students born in the United States should have their tuberculosis skin test done at a local health department or by their private physician one (1) year prior to registration. This must be a mantoux skin test—the Tine test is not acceptable. Any student who has a positive tuberculosis skin test will have a chest X-ray. If the chest X-ray is positive for tuberculosis, the student will be referred to the health department for treatment and will not be permitted to attend class until the possibility of transmitting the disease is no longer present. Students with a positive skin test and a negative chest X-ray will be offered treatment with Isoniazid (an anti-tuberculosis drug) for a period of at least six months. All students not born in the United States (regardless of citizenship) must have a chest X-ray taken in the United States within the past year.

DOCUMENTATION BY A PHYSICIAN OR HEALTH DEPARTMENT FOR THE ABOVE SCREENING IS REQUIRED BEFORE REGISTRATION.

## Immunizations

Immunizations for measles, mumps and rubella (MMR) are required of all students born on or after 1/1/57. Students should have received the first dose of MMR after 12 months of age, and a second dose at least 30 days after the first injection. All students born after 1/1/57 must have documentation of rubella immunization or immunity.

DOCUMENTATION BY A PHYSICIAN OR HEALTH DEPARTMENT OF THESE IMMUNIZATIONS IS REQUIRED.

## Eligibility of Treatment

Students enrolled in classes, co-op students, spouses of students enrolled in classes or the co-op program (if both the student and the spouse have paid their health fees), and continuing education students with a current student ID are eligible for treatment if the health fee is paid.

## Terms of Eligibility

Once the health fee has been paid, students/spouses are eligible for services from the date paid to the end of break week for each quarter, new students are eligible for services during the break week that precedes the quarter they are entering if they can present proof that the fee was paid.

## Cost

A quarterly health fee is automatically assessed to students taking six hours or more. All others must pay the health fee at the health center or present the health center with proof that the health fee has been paid. A $10 late penalty will be assessed if the health fee is paid after the second week of each quarter.

# Special Health Considerations

It is the responsibility of all students to notify the Health Services and the Department of Health and Performance Sciences and the Office of Disabled Services of any disability that would make participation in swimming, competitive sports, and aerobic training hazardous to their well being. Any student requesting special consideration, because of mental or physical disability should have his or her physician write an explanatory letter, giving full details of the disability and consequent limitations on physical activity, to the medical director of the Student Health Center. This letter must accompany the Medical Entrance Form.

Students wanting to continue to receive allergy injections or treatments started by a private physician should enclose a detailed, signed instruction sheet from that physician.

# Health and Accident Insurance

Since the facilities of the Student Health Center are limited, supplemental insurance to cover major illnesses and surgeries, specialist consultations, and diagnostic procedures (not available at the Student Health Center) should be purchased by all students who are not covered by their parents' or spouses' medical insurance plans. As a general rule, private hospitals in the community will not admit patients who do not have hospitalization insurance. Supplemental insurance plans and information are available to students and their dependents. These policies also cover health services while away from campus between quarters, during vacations, during co-op quarters, or during terms not enrolled. PLEASE READ THE POLICY CAREFULLY. IF A MORE COMPREHENSIVE POLICY IS DESIRED, MAKE ARRANGEMENTS WITH A PRIVATE INSURANCE COMPANY.

# THE COOPERATIVE PLAN ⊛ ◦ ⊛ ◦ ⊛ ◦ ⊛ ◦ ⊛ ◦ ⊛ ⊛

Since 1912, Tech has offered two plans of study—the standard four-year plan and a five-year cooperative plan for students who wish to combine practical experience with technical theory.

Approximately 3,700 cooperative students, selected from applicants on the basis of high scholarship, work in about 600 industries throughout the country (as well as a few international assignments), while they complete academic degree programs.

The Cooperative Division offers programs for majors in aerospace, ceramic, chemical, civil, computer, electrical, industrial and systems, materials, mechanical, nuclear and textile and fiber engineering (including textiles and polymer and textile chemistry), and in biology, chemistry, engineering science and mechanics, computer science, earth and atmospheric sciences, mathematics, physics, management, management science, economics, international affairs, industrial design, and society, technology and culture. The academic curriculum are identical to those offered to regular four year students.

The cooperative program offers the student practical experience and insight into human relations, as well as financial assistance. The work experience co-op students receive is a valuable asset to graduates starting out in their chosen professions. Neither college laboratory experience or employment during vacations can take the place of organized co-op training. The plan requires, to a substantial degree, the experience most companies require of their employees before promoting them to positions of responsibility. Work experience may also assist students undecided about their future plans to determine early in their college careers whether they wish to continue in a particular field.

Moreover, daily contact with diverse groups among their fellow employees offers students practical insights into sociology, psychology, economics, and ethics that no textbooks can supply. Finally, students receive compensation for their services from their employers. Although students are not able to earn all of their college expenses, as a rule they can earn more than half.

Students interested in applying for admission to the cooperative plan should contact the Cooperative Division.

# Advanced Placement
# and Credit · · · · · · · · · · · · · · · · · · · · · · ·

Students entering Georgia Tech may receive college credit based on their scores on the College Board Advanced Placement (AP) examinations. A minimum AP score of 3 in American government, comparative politics, mathematics, music theory, or physics, and a score of 4 in biology, chemistry, computer science, economics, English, French, German, Spanish, or history (American and European) is necessary for credit to be awarded.

English and Chemistry credit may also be awarded on the based-upon scores on the College Board SAT II Subject Tests.

Students who have taken any of the tests mentioned above should have their scores sent directly to Georgia Tech by the College Board.

Under certain conditions, the Department of Modern Languages grants up to nine hours of credit for high school language study. For more information, see College Credit for High School Study under the Department of Modern Languages' section of "Curricula and Courses of Instruction" in the Course Catalog.

# Academic Honesty •••••••••••••••••

Academic honesty is the cornerstone of an institution of higher learning. We expect that our students will conduct themselves according to the principles of honesty and integrity. We anticipate that they will obey the rules and regulations of the Institute and act responsibly.

Consequently, we have a strong commitment to maintain and promote uncompromised academic honesty, and when necessary, discipline those who are dishonest. A student initiative, the Academic Honor Code became official Institute policy during the Fall 1996. Students are required to sign an honor agreement acknowledging their awareness of the Code. The objective of the Academic Honor Code is to level the academic playing field for all students while strengthening the level of academic integrity and trust within the Tech community.

## Access to Student Records

Any student, regardless of age, who is or has been in attendance at the Georgia Institute of Technology has the right to inspect and review his or her educational records within a reasonable period of time (not to exceed 45 days) after making a request. "Educational records" means generally any record maintained by or for the Georgia Institute of Technology that contains information directly related to the student. However, the student will not have access to the following:

1. Financial records of parents

2. Confidential letters of recommendation placed in the records prior to January 1, 1975.

3. Letters of recommendation concerning admission, application for employment, or honors for which the student has voluntarily signed a waiver.

Release of personally identifiable information without student consent will be allowed to the following:

1. Institute personnel who have a legitimate educational interest.

2. Officials of other schools where the student seeks to enroll. The student will be notified of the release of such information and will be provided the copy of the record if requested.

3. Representatives of federal agencies authorized by law to have access to educational records and members of the staff of the Board of Regents of the University System of Georgia.

4. Appropriate persons in connection with a student's application for or receipt of financial aid.

5. State and local officials to whom information must be released pursuant to a state statute adopted prior to November 19, 1974.

6. Organizations conducting studies for the Institute.

7. Accrediting organizations.

8. Parents of a dependent student, as defined by the Internal Revenue Code of 1954, as amended.

9. Necessary persons in emergency situations to protect health and safety.

10. Persons designated in subpoenas or court orders.

Students have the right to obtain copies of information contained in their educational records. There is no charge for an official transcript. Records will be released in compliance with a judicial order or lawfully issued subpoena; however, every reasonable effort will be made to notify the student in advance of compliance.

The following types of educational records are maintained on students by the Georgia Institute of Technology:

*Academic records related to admissions and academic performance (transcripts) are maintained in the Office of the Registrar. Academic records are also maintained in the office of the academic dean and within the individual academic departments and schools.*

*Nonacademic records related to housing, fraternity affairs, international students, women students and records that may affect a student's status are kept within the Office of the Vice President for Student Affairs. The office of the Senior Vice President for Administration and Finance maintains student financial records. The Career Services Center maintains records on students who use that office for employment assistance. The Co-op Division maintains records on students enrolled in the co-op education program.*

Any student may present a written request to the registrar or indicate on the student access system that certain directory information not be released. However, requests that directory information be withheld from a written publication must be received in sufficient time to prevent a delay in processing that publication.

When the student and the official responsible for a particular record are unable to resolve questions as to the accuracy of the information contained therein, the student shall have an opportunity for an impartial hearing to challenge the content of his or her record. Challenges to student records should be initiated by the student concerned and directed in writing to the Office of the Registrar.

## DISCLOSURE OF STUDENT RECORDS

The Family Education Rights and Privacy Act of 1974 (Buckley Amendment) requires the Institute to inform the student of the location, type, and content of official records. The student has a right to receive records, receive explanations on them, challenge information and obtain copies of these documents at reasonable costs. In compliance with this law a listing of specific records kept by the various departments of the Institute will be published in revisions of *The Guide to Student Life* each year.

# THE GEORGIA TECH
# PARENTS ASSOCIATION ••••••••••••••

The Parents Association is one of the best ways to play a continuing role in your student's education. The purpose of the Parents Association is to support the various programs at Georgia Tech by promoting better understanding among parents of the Institute's missions and goals.

The Parents Association has an active voice in the operation of Georgia Tech. In addition to their own projects, they have a hand in everything from admissions to housing, parking and campus safety. As a part of the Georgia Tech Alumni Association, the Parents Association has access to a wide range of resources that allow it to work for the benefit of both parents and students. They keep their members informed and up-to-date on Georgia Tech and its activities. By joining the Parents Association you become a partner in your child's education.

Parents Association dues are $40 per family, per year. The membership year is July through June. Membership dues support the Association's many projects, including:

Communications

Student Welfare

Special Events

Recruitment

Parents Fund

Community Relations

Membership dues do more than support Parents Association Projects. You also get subscriptions to *Tech Topics*, the Alumni Association newspaper, and *The Report Card*, the Parents Association newsletter. The Association also sponsors the annual Family Weekend each fall.

To join the Parents Association you can complete an application online at parents@alumni.gatech.edu and you will be billed later or you can call the Parents Association Office at (404) 894-2732.

# Important Phone Numbers ........

All numbers must be dialed using the (404) area code.

## Academic Departments

| | |
|---|---|
| College of Architecture | 894-4885 |
| Computing | 894-3152 |
| Engineering | 894-2972 |
| Ivan Allen | 894-2601 |
| Sciences | 894-3300 |
| Admissions Office | 894-4154 |
| Bookstore | 894-2515 |
| Bursars Office | 894-4618 |
| Campus Information | 894-2000 |

## Campus Ministries

| | |
|---|---|
| Baptist Student Center | 892-6224 |
| Campus Crusade for Christ | 770-422-1839 |
| Catholic Center | 892-6759 |
| Christian Campus Fellowship | 872-3856 |
| Christian Science College Org. | 894-8555 |
| Episcopal Campus Ministry | 881-0835 |
| Fellowship of Christian Students | 347-8299 |
| Hillel Foundation | 727-6490 |
| InterVarsity Christian Fellowship | 770-962-2718 |
| Lutheran Campus Ministry | 873-5760 |
| Presbyterian Student Center | 892-9723 |
| United Methodist | 892-6317 |
| YMCA | 894-4590 |

| | |
|---|---|
| Campus Police | 894-2500 |
| Career Center | 894-2550 |
| Dining Services | 894-2383 |
| Disabled Student Services | 894-2564 |
| Financial Aid | 894-4160 |
| Greek Affairs | 894-9192 |
| Health Center | 894-2584 |
| Housing/Residential Life | 894-2470 |
| Learning Resource Center | 894-1970 |
| Orientation Office | 894-6897 |
| Parents Association | 894-2732 |
| Parking Office | 894-4611 |
| Registrars Office | 894-4150 |
| Student Affairs/Dean of Students Office | 894-2562 |

# Local Hotels/Motels ...........

Atlanta Hilton and Towers
255 Courtland St
Atlanta, GA 30303
404-659-2000

Best Western
160 Spring St
Atlanta, GA 30303
404-688-8600

Comfort Inn
2115 Piedmont Rd
Atlanta, GA 30324
404-876-4365

Days Inn
683 Peachtree St
Atlanta, GA 30308
404-874-9200

Days Inn
2910 Clairmont Road
Atlanta, GA 30329
404-633-8411

Highland Inn
644 N. Highland Avenue
Atlanta, GA 30306
404-874-5756

Holiday Inn
1810 Howell Mill Rd
Atlanta, GA 30318
404-351-3831

Holiday Inn Express
244 North Avenue
Atlanta, GA 30313
404-881-0881

Marriott Marquis
265 Peachtree St
Atlanta, GA 30303
404-521-000

Omni Hotel at CNN Center
100 CNN Center
Atlanta, GA 30335
404-659-0000

Quality Hotel
89 Luckie Street
Atlanta, GA 30303
404-524-7991

Radisson Hotel
165 Courtland and International
 Blvd
Atlanta, GA 30303
404-659-6500

Ramada
70 John Wesley Dobbs Avenue
Atlanta, GA 30310
404-659-2660

Suburban Lodge
1375 Northside Dr
Atlanta, GA 30318
404-350-8102

Wyndam
125 10th St
Atlanta, GA 30309
404-873-4800

# CAMPUS CALENDAR OF EVENTS . . . .

## Academic Calendar 1999–2000

Georgia Tech operates on the semester plan, with the fall and spring terms normally constituting the academic year. A full summer term schedule offers students the opportunity to accelerate their programs by taking four terms per year. Students may enter a course of study or complete their degree requirement and attend a commencement ceremony in any one of the four terms.

The Office of the Registrar prepares and distributes an official Institute calendar for each term. Dates, filing times, deadlines and other information contained in the official calendar supersede previously published information, including dates in this guide. Adherence to the requirements set by the official calendar is the responsibility of the student.

## Summer Term 1999*

| | |
|---|---|
| June 21 | Classes begin |
| June 22 | Late registration |
| July 5 | Holiday |
| July 16 | Last day to drop a course |
| August 6 | Last day of classes |
| August 9 | Final exams begin |
| August 11 | End of term |
| August 13 | Commencement |

*There will be NO freshmen admitted for summer of 1999 only.

# Fall Term 1999

| | |
|---|---|
| August 20–26 | Late registration |
| August 23 | Classes begin |
| October 15 | Last day to drop a course |
| November 26–29 | Thanksgiving Recess |
| December 10 | Last day of classes |
| December 13 | Final exams begin |
| December 18 | End of term, Commencement |

# Spring Term 2000

| | |
|---|---|
| January 7–13 | Late registration |
| January 10 | Classes begin |
| January 17 | Holiday |
| March 3 | Last day to drop a course |
| April 28 | Last day of classes |
| May 1 | Final exams begin |
| May 6 | End of term, Commencement |

# TECH HISTORY AND TRADITIONS ● ● ● ● ● ● ● ● ● ● ● ● ● ● ● ●

The 85 students attending the first day of classes at the Georgia School of Technology in 1888 worked toward a degree in mechanical engineering, the only degree offered. Classes were held in two buildings, including the now famous Tech Tower. That first day of classes signified the beginning of technological education and economic transformation in the agrarian South.

In 1948, the school's name was changed to the Georgia Institute of Technology. Women were admitted in 1952. In 1961 Georgia Tech became the first school in the Deep South to open its doors to African-American students without a court order. Throughout its first century, and into its second, a degree from Georgia Tech has meant quality.

Georgia Tech students study hard, but they know that there is more to life than all night cram sessions and long hours in a chemistry lab. Since the first day of classes in October 1888, Tech students have created light-hearted traditions to counterbalance the academic load. These traditions, perpetuated today by the men and women of Tech, form a distinctive bond among students—a bond that unites the Tech family.

## A Ramblin' Wreck from Georgia Tech

Tech's fight song that begins "I'm a Ramblin' Wreck from Georgia Tech" has contributed significantly to international recognition of Tech's name. An old folk ballad, "The Sons of the Gamboliers," inspired its words and music. The date of the song's introduction on campus is unclear, but the words first appeared in Tech's 1908 yearbook with all the expletives discreetly deleted.

The name Ramblin' Wreck gained widespread recognition in the 1920s when Tech graduates began building mechanical buggies to improve a poor transportation system in South America. As the reputation of these young engineers spread, so did their nickname—the Ramblin' Wrecks from Georgia Tech.

By 1959, the fame of the song was such that Richard Nixon and Nikita Krushchev sang it at their historic meeting in Moscow. The song's copyright, once owned by an early Tech bandmaster named Frank Roman, became the property of ex-Beatle Paul McCartney in 1979 and has subsequently been sold again.

## The Ramblin' Wreck Parade

Every year on homecoming weekend, Tech students flaunt their mechanical inventiveness in the Ramblin' Wreck Parade. This event challenges students to produce outlandish, "mechanical monstrosities" somehow capable of traversing the course up the Hill to the Library parking lot. Begun in 1932 as a traditional road race between Tech and University of Georgia students, the race at that time covered a course from Atlanta to Athens and involved vehicles that were unreliable at best. As cars improved in performance the resulting higher speeds made the road race a safety hazard and forced its cancellation. By the end of World War II, the Ramblin' Wreck Parade had evolved to its present form. Today, it endures as one of Tech's most ingenious traditions.

## George P. Burdell

A legend in his own time, George P. Burdell was created in 1927 as a practical joke. Incoming Freshman Ed Smith received two application forms by mistake. He used one for himself and, on the second, gave the first name and initial of a relative who was the headmaster of his prep school; Ed used the name of his cat for the surname.

By secretly signing Burdell's fictional name as well as his own name on all of his class rolls, Smith developed Burdell into a legitimate student. He even turned in separate exam papers for Burdell changing the handwriting and answers enough to convince many professors that George was actually a student in good standing. In 1930, George P. Burdell received a bachelor's degree from Tech and later a master's degree. During World War II, George continued his education at Harvard University before serving with the Eighth Air Force in England.

## Keeping George Alive

Other creative students, dismayed at the idea of losing this precocious schoolmate, have devised ways to keep George an active participant in the Georgia Tech system. In the spring of 1969, the first quarter that Georgia Tech used completely computerized registration, George beat the system by enrolling in not just a few courses, but in every course the school offered—more than 3,000 credit hours! Though the computer system proved it could not outwit George. In 1986, he was again on the official roster of every course on campus.

With the help of his friends, George spent much of his time writing letters to the editors of various student publications and Atlanta newspapers, subscribing to magazines without paying for them, and applying for major credit cards. He appeared on Tech's 1987 commencement program and was paged at the 1990 Citrus Bowl when Tech beat Nebraska 45–21. At the 1995 inauguration of Tech's 10th president, Wayne Clough, George's name could be found within the inaugural program as one of the distinguished guests.

## Buzz

Although he has existed in his present form since 1985, Buzz is number one in the hearts of Georgia Tech family members. No one is really sure how and when the term "Yellow

Jacket" came into being, although speculation points to the gold and white jackets Tech supporters wore to football games at the turn of the century. Various featureless insects represented the image over the years. The present charismatic Buzz was designed to adapt to all aspects of Tech life, from riding in the Wreck to studying for finals.

## Become Fluent in Tech Talk

More colorful than computer language, and infinitely more practical, Tech special vocabulary is yet another tradition that unifies the Tech family and sets the Tech "team" apart from other schools. Study this glossary, and after a few days you will be able to understand Tech upperclassmen and all of their buzzwords.

### WORD

A general term for any type of information, such as old quizzes or finals, that may be helpful in surviving any professor's course. "What's the word?" or "Did you get word?"

### THE HILL

The area between the Administration Building and the Library. Also used as a general term for members of the administration. "Wonder what the Hill thought about this year's Ramblin' Wreck Parade?"

### PINK PARACHUTES

An old nickname for drop slips allowing you to withdraw from a course before the middle of the quarter without penalty. "Pink Slips" is more commonly used.

### MA TECH

The cherished name used by students and alumni as the personification of Georgia Tech.

## ROTC (Rot-See)

The Reserve Officer Training Corps through which students train for military service.

## The P.O. or "Box"

The student post office in the Student Center. "I'm on my way to check my Box."

## The Tower

The Administration Building Tower embellished with "TECH" in gold and white neon letters.

## The Whistle

The steam whistle that blows to signal class changes at five minutes before each hour. It also blows whenever Tech wins a football game.

## NASA or SST or the Dish

The Space Science and Technology Building. A huge satellite dish is propped in front of it. SST is a more popular reference.

## The V

The Varsity drive-in restaurant. Home of the "naked dog" and F.O. Also known as "The Greasy V."

## GPA, Overall

Cumulative grade point average. "My overall is 4.0. I'll do better next year."

## The House

The living or meeting quarters of a fraternity or sorority. "We have a meeting at the house tonight."

## The Good Word

To Hell with Georgia!

## D-Day or Drop Day

The last day to drop a course without penalty.

## Rats

The traditional description of freshmen.

## Flush Letters

The dreaded letters of rejection from prospective employers. Rejection may also be referred to as "getting flushed," as in "I just got flushed!"

## The Burger Bowl

The grassy area behind West campus dorms and opposite the Tech police station where Greek Week events take place and rugby games are played. It is the former site of a Burger King®.

## The Thrillerdome

The Alexander Memorial Coliseum at McDonald's Center, where basketball games are played.

## The Quiet Side

East side of the Library. "I'll meet you on the quiet side in 10 minutes."

## Loud Side

West side of the Library.

## SAC (Sack)

Student Athletic Complex. SAC Fields refers to the fields behind the complex where intramural sports are held.

## PCS

Printing and Copying Services. Printing office located at 811 Marietta Street where students can make photocopies of their class notes.

## POD

Plant Operations Division (formerly known as Physical Plant). The department that handles the majority of Tech's maintenance needs.

## TA

Teachers Assistant, usually a graduate student.

## Peter's Park

Parking Deck on Bobby Dodd Way that has basketball and tennis courts on top of it.

## OSCAR

On-line Student Computer Assisted Registration. A book listing courses offered each quarter.

## Dead Week

Last week of classes before finals.

## The Fountain

Fountain in front of the Library.

## The Campanile

The bell tower outside the Student Center.

STUD CENTER

The Student Center.

THE 'NIQUE

Nickname for *The Technique*, the student newspaper.

HOME PARK

A neighborhood off 10th Street where many Tech students reside.

THE SONG OF GEORGIA TECH

I'm a Ramblin' Wreck from Georgia Tech
  And a hell of an engineer—
A helluva, helluva, helluva,
  Helluva engineer.
Like all the jolly good fellows,
  I drink my whiskey clear.
I'm a Ramblin' Wreck from Georgia Tech
  And a hell of an engineer.
Oh! If I had a daughter, sir,
  I'd dress her in white and gold
And put her on the campus
  To cheer the brave and bold.
But if I had a son, sir,
  I'll tell you what he'd do—
He would yell "To Hell With Georgia"
  Like his daddy used to do.

Oh! I wish I had a barrel of rum
  And sugar three thousand pounds,
A college bell to put it in,
  And a clapper to stir it 'round.
I'd drink to all good fellows,
  Who come from far and near.
I'm a Ramblin', Gamblin'
  Hell of an engineer.

# LIFE IN ATLANTA ......................

## Cultural Activities

### THE HIGH MUSEUM OF ART

Located at 16th and Peachtree Streets, The High Museum houses an impressive permanent collection and features world class travelling exhibitions. Admission is free on Thursdays.

### ATLANTA SYMPHONY ORCHESTRA

Under the direction of Yoel Levi, the ASO performs regularly in the Woodruff Arts Center (next to The High Museum) during the fall, winter and spring. Student discounts are available at the door 20 minutes prior to each performance.

### THE ALLIANCE THEATER

Also located in the Woodruff Arts Center, the Alliance Theater is stage to both local and international Theater Companies. Student discounts are available for most performances.

### THE ATLANTA BALLET

The Ruth Mitchell Dance Company, and the Dancer's Collective perform in season, along with many touring dance companies that appear year round in Atlanta at various locations around town.

## The Carter Presidential Library

Home of the Carter Foundation, whose focus has been in facilitating the processes of world peace. Various lectures and seminars are offered throughout the year.

## The Martin Luther King, Jr. Center for Nonviolent Social Change

Located on Auburn Avenue, the Martin Luther King, Jr. Center is the location of the tomb of Dr. King. Offering tours as well as seminars throughout the year, the King Center is a crucial instrument for social change in this city.

## Fernbank Science Center

Newly renovated, the Fernbank Science Center features permanent collections on dinosaurs, native Georgia wildlife, and more. Also contains an Imax theater with regular features that rotate throughout the year.

## Other Atlanta Happenings

Scitrek is a science museum located next to the Civic Center on Courtland Avenue.

The World of Coca-Cola® is a museum all about, yes—you guessed it, Coke. Located downtown next to Underground Atlanta.

Underground Atlanta is a shopping district near the Five Points Marta Station. Featuring shops, restaurants and bars.

The Atlanta Botanical Gardens are located off of Piedmont in Midtown.

Oglethorpe University hosts the Georgia Shakespeare Festival every year.

The Virginia Highlands and Little Five Points districts offer unique shops and restaurants ranging from eco-conscious to bohemian.

The Buckhead area, north of Tech is home to Lenox Square and Phipps Plaza shopping malls. Also in Buckhead are various restaurants, clubs and moderate-to-high priced shops and boutiques.

The Atlanta Preservation Center provides walking tours of historic areas and buildings in midtown and downtown Atlanta.